To K[...] [...]l

mama.

with you[...]

your big black angel.

NO GROUND

NO GROUND

Evelyn Carter
with
Leona Choy

Logos International
Plainfield, New Jersey

All Scripture references,
unless otherwise noted,
are taken from The Amplified Bible.

PTL TELEVISION NETWORK
CHARLOTTE. NORTH CAROLINA 28279

MEMO TO: REV EV

MEMO FROM: JIM BAKKER

SUBJECT: RECOMMENDATION FOR READING OF BOOK

Dear Rev Ev:

I would like to say, "I highly recommend NO GROUND
to every person who would like to live a victorious
Christian life. There is no greater joy or pleasure
in life - than to know victory and peace - and to
walk in His ways. May God bless every person who
reads NO GROUND and give them new insights to the
glorious privilege of serving Jesus Christ."

                    In warmest Christian love,

                    James O. (Jim) Bakker,
                    President-PTL Television Network

JOB/re

P. S. I might add: "Rev Ev is one of my favorite
people, and I count it an honor to say a few words
out of my heart for one of my dearest friends."

v

Table of Contents

Foreword

This book breathes the spirit which animates Evelyn Carter. It is simple, yet profound. It teaches without lecturing. It hits the mark of truth but with love. It leaves you standing ten feet tall because the author has brought you into the arms of the Savior.

It has been Evelyn Carter's unique privilege to teach the gospel of Jesus Christ in a way which not only gets to the heart of the matter but is also well-nigh unforgettable. Her voice is still as vivid in my memory today as it was two years ago when I first heard her say, "NO GROUND!" Those words rang out with authority and depth, just as they do in this book.

The intention of this book is to help readers everywhere see themselves with the penetrating and loving eyes of the Master. We are urged to ponder the awesome character of God's humble love which dwells within us, no matter how guilty or unworthy we may feel. The author pleads with us to claim freedom as the children of

God—freed from the bondage of the past. Throughout these pages a bugle of liberty is sounded. When the power of darkness overshadows us, let it be heard: "NO GROUND!" When Satan tempts us toward the slippery paths of doubt and failure, let it be heard: "NO GROUND!" When the subtle and pervasive dangers of arrogance and spiritual pride beckon us, let it be heard: "NO GROUND!" Move on and possess the promised land of redemption and release. Have no fear that the powerful love of God will ever falter or let you go. God's Word is true. His promises do not fail. He will take care of you.

The inspiring message of this book is rooted and grounded in Jesus Christ.

It has been my joy to know Evelyn Carter for many years. We have ministered to needy souls together countless times. I have seen the ministry of deliverance, faith, and hope which she performs with boundless integrity and effectiveness. Her book is a true mirror of her own unique, Christ-filled self. There is a blessing awaiting you on every page. Read them, and live them as Evelyn Carter does.

Joseph P. Bishop, Minister
The Presbyterian Church
Rye, New York

Introduction

"NO GROUND!" is a battle cry that I have adopted and adapted to my life. This book is a correlation between the Scriptures I have learned and their application to daily living.

Victory has been the end result of learning to use the simple phrase—"NO GROUND!" Once you learn the reality of its power, it will become common to you.

"NO GROUND!" has become a weapon I use against the enemy of my soul, as I declare who and what I am through Jesus Christ. May you read it prayerfully.

"Rev. Ev"

NO GROUND

1

ROOTS IN OUR GROUND

The Lord impressed upon me, "Tell my people I'm giving them a new battle cry."

"What is that, Lord?" I asked Him.

"NO GROUND! Tell them not to give the enemy of their souls ANY GROUND!"

"Is that in your Word?"

"My servant, the apostle Paul, told you, 'Leave no [such] room or foothold for the devil—give no opportunity to him' " (Eph. 4:27).

"Hallelujah! How can we do that, Lord?"

"That's what we're going to learn together!"

The Lord Jesus Christ never commanded us to do anything that we cannot do—through Him. Nor anything which He did not do first as our example. "Whoever says he abides in Him (Christ) ought to walk in the same way as He walked" (1 John 2:6, paraphrase).

Jesus gave NO GROUND to the devil because the devil

had NO GROUND in Him. "For the prince (evil genius, ruler) of the world is coming. And he has no claim on Me—he has nothing in common with Me, there is nothing in Me that belongs to him, he has no power over Me" (John 14:30). "As I was in the world, so are ye," He assures.

I fly a lot—in planes, that is. When there's a short layover at a certain city to pick up passengers, sometimes they let continuing passengers get off and go into the lounge awhile. But you want to keep your own seat. So the airline puts a sticker or sign on your seat. It has a block figure of a person with a line drawn across it and the word "Occupied" underneath it and no one else dares to sit there.

That's what NO GROUND is all about. The Christian is Jesus' property. Jesus lives in him—He occupies him. When the enemy comes along looking for a place to sit, the believer has the authority to put up the "Occupied" sign. The devil has no seat. He has NO GROUND in the believer. Hallelujah!

Our commitment to Jesus' lordship should be total from the time we are born again. But in practice, and as we grow in the Lord, Jesus keeps uncovering areas in our lives that we have not let Him occupy. These are potential places for the devil to GET GROUND. If the enemy tries to sit down on a corner of our seat, or step on a piece of Jesus' property, (that's us!) we have to watch out for him. We need to learn how to use our position and authority in Jesus to declare to the enemy, "NO GROUND—you didn't have ANY GROUND in Jesus, and you have NO GROUND in me—scat! I'm going to be like Jesus!"

But the enemy of our souls mocks us, "No way can you

be like Jesus."

But that is not what the Word of God says, nor what Jesus said. He gave no commandment that cannot be carried out. John said, "He who lives in you is greater (mightier) than he who is in the world" (1 John 4:4). Jesus has given us "the authority and power . . . over all the power that the enemy [possesses]" according to Luke 10:19. If He has given us *that*, then the thing we need to learn is *how to use it*.

We are going to go through some heavy and wonderful Bible teaching together in this book. But praise Jesus, *you'll* be different when we finish—I just know it! Hang in there and let's go!

The reason we don't have any more victory than we have is because our minds tell us that it is absolutely impossible. We haven't learned to think like Jesus taught us to think because we are still fragmented people. We are not whole. "If any person is (ingrafted) in Christ, the Messiah, he is (a new creature altogether)" (2 Cor. 5:17). And as new creatures, we have new minds, new emotions, new passions, and new desires. Everything in us must become reconciled to the lordship of Jesus Christ.

But *we* must make the choice to be reconciled. By that I mean, when I see a truth in the Scriptures, which God, by the Spirit, reveals, I can either accept that truth or not. Most of the time I do accept it on an intellectual basis. After that I must choose to believe it—that's an act of my will. Then I have to bring my emotions up to the level of the truth that I've been taught in order that I might develop.

We can quote Scripture about victory and believe it.

3

But emotionally we may still be defeated because we feel there is absolutely no way we can ever attain it. Therefore we are fragmented. And the whole of us—the mind, the will, and the emotions—is not united. We reason with ourselves, I want this to be the truth and I'm striving and struggling to make this become the truth; but after all, I'm only human. We get defeated right at this point.

The Lord showed me a truth—that I had not yet given Him my actions and my reactions. Very glibly and freely I said, "Okay, you can have them, Lord." I agreed with God intellectually, I chose to obey, now God went into action to test me and bring my emotions up to the level of that truth.

He said, "Well then, Evelyn, try it out. You go ahead and react."

And I said, "All right." Now let me tell you what happened.

I had to go away from my home in Pittsburgh about seventy miles to speak at a women's meeting. I was asking the Lord all week for a message. Have you ever prayed and the heaven got brass? That is a black term. In our church we often say, "Heaven gets brass." In other words, when you pray, your prayers seem to go up and bounce right back down—no answer; they just keep resounding. Well, I began to pray and seek the Lord and heaven seemed like brass. I sought Him one day and nothing happened; I sought Him another day and nothing happened. But I have learned that God doesn't have to say anything until He gets good and ready.

That doesn't get me off the hook, though. I had to keep

4

doing my homework, praying, searching the Scriptures, studying, and putting stuff in so that the Lord could pull it out when I needed what I needed—which was Friday.

I was studying in Ephesians, one of my favorite books, and had reached chapter six. I've taught on that many times. In the translation I was using there were these words: "We wrestle not against flesh and blood, nor principalities or powers, but master spirits and wickedness in high places" (6:12). Offhand, I asked, "Lord, what is a master spirit?" Heaven was still brass and He apparently didn't hear me, or at least He didn't say He did. So I let it go at that.

Friday morning came and God still hadn't said anything. But that didn't mean I didn't have to keep my appointment. I have learned to get dressed and put myself together and get myself where I'm supposed to be and expect *Him* to be there and do what *He's* supposed to do when I get there.

Pennsylvania has rolling hills and mountains and two-lane highways and a lot of no-passing zones. I had to take a particular highway and I generally don't mind driving. And I like to drive well—to me, that means fast. At that time I had a nice, big, heavy car. (I always felt that because I was big, I needed big things.) It had a 440 engine in it, so it gave me all the horses I needed. It responded very easily to the pat of my foot. The speed limit was still sixty-five miles an hour, so that meant to me that I could go seventy. I used to do ninety and on up, on occasion, and prayed a crazy prayer: "Dear Jesus, please put blinders on the state troopers while I go down this highway." You better believe that the Lord soon convicted me that I was asking Him to blind somebody so I could break the law. I repented and asked God to help me get my heavy foot off the gas pedal and He did—with my cooperation.

That morning I got on a clear stretch of highway—and behind the worst man driver I have ever got behind in my life! In a fifty mile zone, he was doing ten. God was giving me the privilege of reacting.

So I immediately, if not sooner, reacted. I got mad. I got good and mad. I had not allowed myself to get mad for ten years because "good Christians don't get mad." But now I got so mad that it was like being consumed in white heat!

I said, "Well, Lord, Merlin Carothers says I'm supposed to praise you in *all* things. So—thank you, Jesus. Glory to God. Hallelujah. Amen. And I'm still mad!" I said, "Lord, I just gave you some lip service, but please, Holy Spirit, help me to really praise Jesus."

I have a prayer language, and when I asked the Holy Spirit to help me genuinely pray, the norm for me would have been to break out in my prayer language. To my utter amazement, out of my mouth came, "Dear Jesus, just like that man is lost. . . ."

Now I was in my own car behind that man with no communication between us. There was no way I could know he had lost his direction. One of the gifts of the Spirit had gone into operation, the gift of knowledge, because in the natural, I couldn't have known that the man was lost. And I said, "Lord, just like that man is lost, so are many souls lost on the highway of life. Please, dear Jesus, allow me the privilege of being a road sign on the way of life to point people to the Way, which is yourself, Lord."

And with that, the Lord spoke to me. He finally broke the silence of the whole week. But when He did, I thought He changed the subject. "Evelyn," He said, "you are an illegitimate child."

And I said, "What else is new? I've known that for X number of years."

The Lord continued, "But Evelyn, there *are no* illegitimate children. I am the Father of all life and there is not a child that is born into the world to whom I do not give life and become his or her Father. I have written in my Word that I am the God of the fatherless." He went on to explain to me, "There are promiscuous parents but no illegitimate children." And with that, the dear gentleman driver disappeared—car, man, and everything disappeared! To this day I wonder whether he might not have been an angel sent from God!

I started whizzing down the highway—free at last. And the Lord kept speaking to me, "You know, Evelyn, when you were a little girl, you started out to be a very happy little girl. That is, until you began to walk into certain groups, and people began to whisper behind their hands and make you feel uncomfortable. You began to look at yourself to see if your slip was showing or something didn't look right. And then you found out that *you* were different from other little children because they all had daddies who lived in their houses and you didn't. You didn't want to be different, so you told a lie.

"Your mother had told you that good little girls don't lie, so then you began to feel guilty about lying. As you got older and began to understand things, you began to resent your mother for putting you in the position of having to

7

lie." And He continued, "You became full of resentment and bitterness—and SHAME."

What the Lord had brought up was true. I had purposed in my heart that I wanted to be a *mother* to my future children like my mother was to me; but I never wanted to be the *woman* that my mother was because I was the eldest of five illegitimate children. I hated her for the woman that she was, but loved her for the dynamic mother that she was, doing the best she could under bad circumstances. I purposed in my heart that *I* was not going through life on my back. So, of course, I ended up with a lot of sexual hang-ups that led to a whole bunch of other things.

But the Lord said to me, "Ev, we have got rid of the resentments, and the anger, and the bitterness, and the frustration in some areas of your life. . . ." And as He talked to me, there seemed to appear a huge wheel in the center of my sight. He said, "You asked me what a master spirit was." (And here I thought He hadn't even been listening to me!) "We have been working on the *spokes* of the wheel—the resentment, bitterness, and those things, but Ev, we have never dealt with the *hub* of the wheel."

And I said, "What's the hub, Lord?"

And He said, "You asked me what a master spirit was. In *your* life, SHAME is one of the biggest master spirits out of the pit of hell." And He said, "What did *you* have to do to get born?"

And I admitted, "Nothing, Lord."

He said, "Then why should *you* be ashamed all of your life?"

And with that, it seemed that two hands went down

8

into the core of my being and scooped out the biggest jelly-mass you have ever seen, with all kinds of tentacles on it. And the Lord said, "Ev, I've brought you to the place in me that I can remove this. I've wanted to do that for a long time, but you would have resisted me and one of those tentacles would have broken off, only to grow again."

And with that, God's hands seemed to lift the whole gloppy mass out of me. And as that mass came up, I was released with joyful cries, yells, hollers, and I whooped for the last forty miles with the greatest relief of my life—but still with no message for my meeting.

The fantastic part of it was that when I had reacted in anger to that slow driver, something had begun to happen. I searched my heart, "Lord, I am reacting. But what am I reacting to?" Then I discovered that I was not reacting to *that man*. To what then?

I had been taught all my life that white people thought black people were always late for everything. And I purposed in my heart, when I found out God was calling me to a ministry to white people, that *I* would always be on time; and, in fact, *ahead of time*. And I would wait on *them* and they would *never* have to wait on me. I didn't realize this fully; it was a subconscious thing.

Here was a man going ten miles an hour and I still had seventy miles to go and *I would be late*! Beside that, I was anxious because I didn't have any message. And all those women (the neighborhood to which I was going was ultra-ultra) were sure to be sitting there *waiting* and *this man* was making me late. And I reacted unconsciously to the fact that those white people were going to think that

here was another one of those late black people who was
trifling with them.

When I was free enough to deal with my reaction, I
discovered its roots. God had to dig all the way down to
uncover SHAME. I had been GIVING GROUND all my
life to shame. I never felt I was good enough to measure
up. I always figured I had to compensate because of the
circumstances of my birth.

By this time I had arrived at the meeting place (I
burned up the highway, by the way) and came barreling
into the house as only I can do. Sure enough, those nice
ladies had been sitting there waiting very patiently for me
(because I *was* late) with their little coffee cups and
twisting their hankies and the whole shmere.

But I was feeling so free! And I went to running off my
mouth quickly and sharing with them about shame and
what the Lord had just taught me. As I shared, suddenly
one fashionable woman sitting in a corner began to scream
with joy, "I'm *not* responsible for my promiscuous mother
either!" And another one exclaimed, "*I'm* not responsible
for my drunken father!" And so it began to ricochet back
and forth across the room because these dear people, too,
had been bound in their emotions to one of the same
master spirits—shame. And they too had GIVEN
GROUND to the enemy year after year, some for all their
lives, to something they were not even conscious of. And
it just blew my mind! What a message the Lord had
quietly been preparing within me to give!

Then God said, "Evelyn, when I called Lazarus out of
the grave, he came out like a redeemed man, but he was
bound. Many of my people are redeemed but bound

emotionally to the past: mothers who didn't love their sons and never cuddled them; daughters whose fathers never took them on their laps or had rejected them at age five, or ceased to embrace them or teach them by example how to normally relate to a man and such things. Many are bound by fear; others by puritanical backgrounds."

We haven't all had religious parents and even if they were religious, *they* may have been bound by their backgrounds and they passed their hang-ups on to us. Many of us are redeemed but bound.

And Jesus said, "Ev, I had to tell a *man* to loose the *man* and set him free." A man had bound Lazarus, and a man had to unbind him. Do you understand that?

And God said, "I want my people to know that they don't have to GIVE GROUND to the past, or to their hang-ups." Jesus Christ was hung on the cross for our hang-ups. Hallelujah!

Now I was free to pray, "Jesus Christ, I thank you that you love me enough to reveal the places in my life where I've been GIVING GROUND to the enemy. I want to take up the battle cry NO GROUND and lay myself open to you!"

And when *you* pray that too, the Lord will get to work on the master spirits and the roots in *your* life that you need to have dug out!

2

OUR GROUND
FOR *NO GROUND*

Have you seen those switchable signs on motels as you
drive along the highway? They read either "Vacancy" or
"No Vacancy." What they spell out determines whether
you decide to turn into their driveway or not, if you are
looking for a room.

The Christian should hang a permanent "No Vacancy"
sign on all areas of his life because he has the *Holy* Spirit
dwelling in him. When the devil drives by, he knows he
has no welcome there—NO GROUND. No use to even
turn into the driveway of our lives or knock at the door.
But if there is any uncommitted, unsurrendered area in
our lives, it is like hanging the "Vacancy" sign out and
inviting the enemy to come in with his dirty feet all over
God's clean carpet. Consciously or unconsciously, we've
put out the welcome mat for the devil and we are in for
trouble.

Let's look at Jesus for our example of keeping the
enemy off the premises. In Jesus Christ, humanity and

divinity are one. I think that the most glorious thing in the Scriptures is the integration of those two natures in Jesus. Though He was 100 per cent man and 100 per cent God, He took His divinity, wrapped it up in flesh, and brought it into subjection to the flesh. He made the choice that the Father should be the originator of every thought and every desire; He reconciled the whole of himself mentally and emotionally, by an act of His will, to the truth that had been revealed to Him.

He was the Son of God and at the same time He walked the earth as a man; everything on earth responded to Him because there was no fragmentation in Him. He never once thought that He couldn't do what the Father said He could do. So He went about doing. He was totally possessed with the will to do the Father's will. He said, "My food (nourishment) is to do the will (pleasure) of Him Who sent Me and to accomplish and completely finish His work" (John 4:34).

As a new creature in Christ Jesus, the law of my new being is also to do the will of my Father. Jesus declared that nothing in Him belonged to the devil so He had nothing to fear from him. The devil could not get a piece of ground to put his foot on in Jesus (John 14:30). Why could He say this? Because Jesus Christ accomplished His miracles as a man filled with the power of God. Jesus opened blind eyes—as a man; He raised the dead—as a man; He made the dumb talk—as a man. He gave us a living example of how every man who is in right relationship with God the Father, filled with the Holy Spirit, living in this world, ought to act. That makes us, according to the Word, debtors to do just like He did.

Why? Because a *man* showed us how to do it.

So when the enemy of our souls comes along and says, "You can't do it," we should answer, "There's a man, the man Jesus Christ, who's now sitting at the right hand of the Father, to whom the angels must give obedience, who is receiving the glory that He had with the Father before. He walked the earth as a man. Therefore *I* can do what He did. He did not fear the enemy, so I don't either. Though He was tempted in every point just like I am, *He* did not yield and neither do *I* have to!" Jesus never relied on himself. His will was to do the will of the Father. He kept turning to God moment by moment in every situation, never thinking that He could handle anything apart from the Father. So it is our privilege to turn to Him moment by moment.

What happens when self comes up? Don't we realize that we have been crucified? Unless we're crucified, we don't have life. We were on the cross in Christ. The Scripture says, "Consider yourselves also dead to sin" (Rom. 6:11). Our new life is "hid with Christ in God" (Col. 3:3). Do you realize what that means? If our life is hid in God through Christ Jesus, the blood is there as a witness. The shed blood of Jesus stands as a perpetual sign that we've been purchased and belong to God. There is the blood—there is the Lord Jesus Christ—and the Holy Spirit—then God, the Father, is behind it all and we're locked up inside Him. Everything has to come through *each of them* in order to get at us! No wonder the enemy of our souls does not want us to realize that truth. Do you understand now why we have been commanded to give the enemy NO GROUND and no foothold and no

15

opportunity and no place?

We are to give him NO GROUND to stand on—mentally, emotionally, academically, socially, physically, morally, not in any way to give him opportunity in our lives. Anything that you lay claim to—anything that you say, "This is mine," is GROUND for the enemy. You are no longer your own, Paul said. You've been bought with a price and that price was the shed blood of Jesus Christ on Calvary.

It all begins with *knowing who you really are*. If you know that, and trust the One to whom you yielded your life, and know who *He* is, then you can be what you are supposed to be and do what you are supposed to do.

I think one of the most releasing thoughts is that God is *obligated* to us. That might be kind of mind-blowing. *God is obligated to you*. Who do you think you are that God would be obligated to you? But if you know who you are—a child of God—then God is your Father. Any father is obligated to his children to provide for them, isn't he? And who is God? God is our Father.

The Scripture says that we should call Him "Abba." And "Abba" is an Aramaic word borrowed from childhood that corresponds in some ways to our word, "daddy." To me there is a difference between a daddy and a father. There's an intimacy that you have with a daddy that you don't quite have with a father. When little children climb on their father's lap and have a really close relationship, they call him "daddy." But when they grow up, they start becoming very formal and stand back from him. They aren't little cuddly kids any more. Personally, I kind of like to say "daddy" to God. If we know who we are, we can

16

have that kind of intimate relationship.

Then I need to get my mind set on the truth that I don't have to give in to anything that is not like the nature of my heavenly daddy. We have become partakers and sharers of the divine nature of God (2 Pet. 1:4). When we received Jesus Christ as our personal Lord and Savior, He took that old nature and nailed it to the cross and put in its place His very own nature. That is what makes us bone of His bone and flesh of His flesh. He impregnates us with His characteristics within us and then puts us into situations in life that will help us to develop those characteristics. Our new mind-set has to be that we *don't* have to give the enemy ANY GROUND.

It never entered the head of Jesus that He was going to be a failure. It never entered the mind of Christ that He was separated from His Father. Once it was revealed to Him who He was—that He was the Son of God—He brought all His intuitiveness, His thinking, His feelings, His emotions, His will, His desires, and aligned them all with the truth that had been revealed to Him. Then He walked and accomplished exactly what the Father said He could.

We go through the act of being born again and accepting Jesus Christ as our personal Savior. We do this mentally; we do this by choice. But then we don't bring our emotions up to that level and we live defeated lives. We are fragmented; the whole of us can't say that we won't give the devil ANY GROUND. We reason, "I know that is what the Scripture says; I accept that. Yes, I choose not to give the devil ANY GROUND. But down in my emotions I can't grasp it—that's too big for me. The devil has more power than I have." That's a lie! Christian, *you* have more power than the devil has. Why? Because Jesus Christ gave you power *over* him. You have to have your mind changed so that you can begin to think like a joint heir with Christ Jesus.

Are you afraid? Do you know what fear is? Fear is perfect faith in failure! It is the total belief that I can't do anything but fail. If you have this perfect faith in failure, the enemy can totally strip you because you'll never try to accomplish anything. Do you see how the enemy attacks us? Through the mind.

We cannot stop the negative thoughts from coming. But we don't have to entertain them; we don't have to play with them, nor handle them. If you know that negativity is not the nature of God, you don't have to deal with it. I don't mean that you should keep repeating, "Now I can't be negative; I can't be negative!" You've already given GROUND. The enemy already has your attention. In James 4:7 it says, "So be subject to God.—Stand firm against the devil; resist him and he will flee from you." Do you know that you will be victorious if you simply don't pay any attention to him?

It is very plain what the enemy wants to do. He comes to do three things: to steal, to rob, and to destroy (John 10:8, 10). He comes to steal your *attention*, rob your *affections*, and destroy your *energy*. He steals our attention by getting our minds and our wills off Jesus. The thing he puts our attention on when he gets it off Jesus is *ourselves*. When we start to worry about ourselves he has our attention. Second, he comes to rob our affection. It follows that whatever has your attention will get your affection. Third, he destroys our energy by draining us emotionally.

Medical science is finding out more and more about the underlying cause of diseases. Previously doctors thought the root causes were in the mind. Now they are discovering that it isn't actually in the mind, it's in the spirit of the man. See what has happened? They have only been dealing with two aspects of man—the physical and the mental. Man is a tripartite being—body, mind, and spirit. What they have neglected is the spirit of the man. In fact, man is basically spirit, because man's life stems from the Spirit of God.

Do you see what Jesus came to do? He bridged the gap and brought the spirit into ascendancy and put man back into relationship with his God. In the *body* we have the senses, the place of world consciousness because the world touches man through his senses. This is the outer portion of us. Then the *mind* houses the emotions and the will as well as the conscience. The mind is the center of self-consciousness. The *spirit* is the place of God-consciousness. Worship and prayer are born in the spirit of the man.

When a person is born again, something happens—a transfer takes place. The body, or the world-consciousness, and the spirit, or the God-consciousness, switch place in prominence. The inner life becomes the greatest and most important part of the person. Man becomes conscious of God and has a desire to pray and have fellowship with his Maker.

Notice that the mind does not change its place; the self-consciousness does not change its place. The will and emotions also stay in their same place, as does the intellect. Why? Because God ordained that the mind should be the avenue through which the inner and the outer worlds are reached. And whoever controls the mind controls the man. That's why the mind is the great battlefield.

So many people say, "After all, I have a good mind; God gave me a good mind." It may be true. In the western world we've developed the mind to the neglect of the spirit. We've begun to worship the creature more than the Creator. The mind was the creation of God and we've begun to worship it more than we worship the One who created it. We've neglected that very portion of our lives that would keep us in tune with Him.

When we receive Jesus Christ as our Lord and Savior, our spirits are quickened (made alive) and we are brought back into our relationship with God who is spirit. Then the spirit becomes the predominant part of us. Without the spirit we cannot communicate with God because "God is a Spirit (a spiritual Being) and those who worship Him must worship Him in the spirit and in truth (reality)" (John 4:24). We can know much *about* God, and we can make a mental assent to Him, but we can never enter into relationship with Him except by the Spirit of God. We cannot have fellowship with God except by the Spirit. Our spirits have to be quickened and awakened and brought into fellowship with Him.

Many people come to know the Lord but they never get around to developing a relationship with Him. They are on the right side of the cross, but not on the right side of the resurrection. It is only when we deal with the resurrected Christ and hunger and thirst after Him that we go on to receive the infilling of the Holy Spirit. Then the Holy Spirit helps us to want to know Him more and fellowship with Him. Paul had been preaching for fourteen years, then one day he was consumed with the reality of knowing Jesus more deeply. He said, "I want to know Him, I want to become more deeply and intimately acquainted with Him. . . . I want to know Him in the power outflowing from His resurrection which it exerts over believers" (Phil. 3:10, paraphrase). "Even while in the body," he adds. Not pie in the sky by-and-by.

It is the Holy Spirit who reveals Jesus Christ in depth. "When He, the Spirit of Truth (the truth-giving Spirit) comes, He will guide you into all the truth—the whole, full truth" (John 16:13). Some truth? Occasional truth? Truth every now and then? No—*all* truth!

First John 2:20 says that we have an unction from the Holy One and we *know the truth*. The devil says, "You don't know nothin'!"

So we GIVE HIM GROUND and say, "Yes, that's right, I *don't* know anything; how can I possibly know God?"

But God says, "You have an anointing, an unction through which *you know all things*." It is by the Holy Spirit, the Spirit who brought everything into existence. God spoke, the Spirit moved, and there was. There was nothing made that the Spirit of God was not in on or did not cause to be brought about because the Holy Spirit is the action part of the Godhead. The Holy Spirit is the enabler, the empowerer of the believer. He is not only *with*, not only *upon*, but *in* the believer. When we receive Jesus Christ,

21

the Spirit of God enters into our spirits and our spirits become the source of all spirituality. Out of us begin to issue the things of eternal life and we are on our way. Hallelujah!

3

THAT OLD WOOL PULLER

The enemy of our souls is an expert at pulling the wool over our eyes. He wants to keep us blindfolded to what we really are in Christ and what we have in Christ. He keeps telling us: "You can't know the things of God; you should keep your old value system—it served you well." One of the basics of that old mind-set is to constantly look outside of ourselves for our direction and strength.

But the truth is that the life-giving Spirit has become resident *within* us; we should stop seeking for things outside and start tuning in on the inside. We must start taking our direction from the inward man because there is the seat and heart of God.

According to 1 Corinthians 2:11, no man knows another man except by the spirit of the man. We have not been given the spirit of the world, but we have been given the Spirit of God that we might know the things that are freely and lavishly given to us by God.

"What eye has not seen, and ear has not heard, and has

not entered into the heart of man, [all that,] God has prepared—made and keeps ready—for those who love Him. . . . Yet to us God has unveiled and revealed them by and through His Spirit, for the (Holy) Spirit searches diligently . . . the profound and bottomless things of God" (1 Cor. 2:9, 10). The Holy Spirit's delight is to reveal the will of the Father to us. Who am I to think that I could know the things of God? The Scripture is clear, He has given us His Spirit (Eph. 3:16) and now we *are able* to know the love of God. How else could I comprehend it? With my finite mind, I couldn't possibly fathom the love of God. The Scripture says that by His Spirit we *can* know that love of God in its breadth, its length, its height, and its depth (Eph. 3:18). That's the totality of the love of God! We can know the fullness of the love of God while we're still in our bodies because it is the Holy Spirit's desire to reveal the love of God to us.

Paul asks us whether anything could separate us from that love of God (Rom. 8:35-39). He answers, "I'm persuaded beyond doubt." That's the kind of assurance that the Holy Spirit will give you. I always say that every believer needs his B.A., his D.D., and his P.H.D. He needs to be Born Again, a Devil Disturber, and Past Having Doubts! James describes the man who is doubtful as being like the waves of the sea, double-minded, and so not able to receive anything.

But Paul says, "I am persuaded beyond doubt—am sure—that neither death, nor life, nor angels, nor principalities, nor things impending and threatening, nor things to come, nor powers, nor height, nor depth, nor anything else in all creation will be able to separate us from the love of God" (Rom. 8:38, 39).

"In all creation" includes the devil! We can't get so far that the love of God can't find us; we can't get so low that the love of God can't get that deep; we can't get so high that the love of God can't reach us; we can't get so far afield that the love of God can't touch us. There can be wars but in the midst of them God's love can find us. Men can't explode enough bombs or make enough smoke screens to keep God's love from going through. To me, that's victory! That should cause joy to start springing up in your heart! There's not a sin that can separate me from the love of God either. Why? Because God cares more about me than I do myself.

That is real security, even *eternal security* because God's Word is eternal. I don't mind being eternally secure, do you? This is not some denomination's doctrine; it is the Word of God. It's just absolutely fantastic that there is nothing in all creation for eons and eons of ages that will ever separate us from the love of God. That slaps the devil right in his face.

Another wool blindfold the enemy tries to fasten on us is the threat of separation from God—that we can do something to cause God to reject us. But the blood of Jesus is perpetually there as a witness to our salvation. I deserved to be punished for my wrongdoing but He said "I'll pay the price instead." Now every time we do something for which we need to be punished, not only is Jesus sitting at the right hand of the Father, but the blood is there eternally on the mercy seat. If the Father should rise up in wrath, all Jesus would have to say is, "Hey, Dad," and God would turn and look at His Son and there

He would see *my security* in Jesus' blood. That's exciting to me!

"The sheep that are My own hear and are listening to My voice, and I know them and they follow Me. And I give them eternal life, and they shall never lose it or perish throughout all the ages—to all eternity they shall never by any means be destroyed. And no one is able to snatch them out of My hand" (John 10:27, 28). Isn't that exciting? God the Father said in the Old Testament that He has engraved us on the palms of His hands. We have become etched into His very essence so that the substance of our being is the very nature of God. He can't lose us if we are an integral part of himself.

He also assures us that He forgives us of our sins in Psalms 32:1, 2 and repeats it in Romans 4:7, 8. In Hebrews 10 he declares the absolute remission of our sins. And our law breakings shall He remember no more because they are completely buried and covered up. So I just figure that if God isn't keeping any account of my sin, why should I waste my time doing so? That may sound too simple but that's just the way it is. If it's no big thing to God, and He has no records, then I think the devil has a whole lot of nerve to keep records that God doesn't keep!

Do you see why the enemy keeps the record of our sins? It is to poke at you when you try to do something good. The devil will say, "Remember when you did this or did that?" You are reminded, agree with the enemy and you GIVE HIM GROUND because now he has your attention. He starts condemning you and you just stand there and take it because you don't know that "Therefore there is *now no condemnation* . . . for those who are in

Christ Jesus" (Rom. 8:1). Aren't you in Christ? God said
He engraved you on His hands. And what my Daddy has
in His hand, no man can pluck out. "My Father and I are
one," Jesus said. So if I'm in Jesus' hand and He is in me,
we are one. Since the devil couldn't do anything with
Jesus before, how is he going to do anything with Jesus in
me?

You see, we keep forgetting who we are. We accept it
intellectually and by choice but our emotions still say,
"Now I've got to work and labor to measure up to that
kind of reality." No, I have to *accept* that reality first and
by an act of my will bring up my emotions to believe the
truth so that I can begin to walk in the way He says I
ought to. It's just that simple.

We know that everything we receive from God is
two-way: God does His part and then I do my part. God
has revealed to us by the Spirit through the Scriptures
and by the apostles what we have in Jesus; it is up to us to
claim it. And if we claim it, then it is up to us to act like it.
If someone left you $100,000 and all you had to do was to
go get it, which you did, but then never got around to
spending—that's *your* problem. It's not that you don't
have it, it's not that it is not available. You may continue
to live like a pauper even though the resources are there
to open up a whole new way of life for you. You have it but
you're just not applying it, or appropriating it or using it.

That is exactly what is happening in the body of Christ.
We have not appropriated what has been given to us. In
most of our churches we are taught that salvation is the
biggest thing. We are encouraged to come to the cross.
That is certainly necessary and good but we are *not*

taught the fellowship of the cross or how to live and walk in the life of Christ. "Get saved!"—that's all the church emphasizes. There is an extended purpose in the cross of Christ: Jesus first lived and showed us how we ought to live; then He died to secure it for us. Therefore we're debtors to Him to live it out. He's sitting at the right hand of the Father to reveal heaven in us here on the earth. He taught us how to live on the earth as sons and joint heirs of God but *we* have to bring everything in us up to that reality and not tolerate anything beside that.

Jesus never went to any funeral and said, "I sure would like to raise this dead man but I can't. I don't have enough power." Do we reason like that? "What would my pastor say? What would my husband say? What would my mother say if that person really got up?" Can you imagine Jesus standing before Lazarus wondering, "God, do you think I can do it? Oh, I don't know what these townspeople will think. I don't know what the church fathers would say." They were all out there, the Pharisees, the Sadducees, the church leaders of that day. Can you just picture Jesus saying, "Oh, I'm so nervous. What if I call him and he *doesn't* get up?" You can't? But you can picture *yourself* doing something like that!

But the same Jesus, the *same* Jesus who called Lazarus out of the grave, who had the power by the spoken word to say, "Lazarus, come forth!" and life was quickened anew in his body and he *came* forth—that *same* Jesus is resident within us. He has the same power, the same ability, the same energy He had before and *He is in us*, but He is blocked by our mind-set. Because the wool puller, the enemy of our souls, says, "Who do *you* think you are?" Who *do* I think I am? Well, you should tell him who you are!

What happens when you start telling him who you are? What happens when you start lifting up Jesus to the enemy? What happens to the enemy? You get lost praising the Lord and thinking about who you are. You get the victory, don't you? The only way Satan can defeat you is if he can keep you from knowing and confessing who you are and what the Word says. You overcome *by the Word* of your testimony and the blood of the Lamb.

Paul says, "I have strength for all things in Christ Who empowers me . . . Who infuses inner strength into me, [that is, I am self-sufficient in Christ's sufficiency]" (Phil. 4:13). In the midst of any crisis you are more than a conqueror. Some people in history get to be conquerors. But Paul says, "You are *more* than a conqueror." How? "Through Jesus Christ who loves us."

But Paul says, "GIVE NO GROUND!" That is *our* responsibility. If you know who you are, you don't have to accept defeat. Defeat is not of the nature of God. There is no defeat in Jesus. There is no defeat in the Holy Spirit. So if we are infused with the Father, the Son, and the Holy Spirit, there ought not be any defeat in us! If we allow the Spirit of God to have the preeminence and fill the whole of our lives, our emotions, passions, desires, will, reason, and everything else, there won't be any room for the enemy. We don't have to give him ANY GROUND.

Jesus told us to take hold of our possessions. The wool puller tries to keep us from doing so. What hinders us? Actually, there's nothing capable of hindering you. Nothing hindered Jesus and as He was, you are. If you are a born-again believer, then He has secured your salvation and His victory becomes your victory. "[The Father] has delivered and drawn us to Himself out of the control and the dominion of darkness" (Col. 1:13). If I'm delivered from that, it does not have power over me. Why should I fear it? I've been delivered! I have been "transferred . . . into the kingdom of the Son of His love."

Before I knew Christ, I was under the dominion of the enemy. There are only two classifications in the world—saint or sinner. You are either in Christ or out of Christ. If you are out of Christ, you are under the persuasion of the enemy. But if you are in Christ, you are under the lordship of Jesus Christ and under *His* power. The Word says delivered *out of* and *to*: delivered out of the power of one, into the power of the other. That takes us from being underdogs to being chiefs! That is a direct exchange from *under* to *over*. That makes you the boss!

The Father has brought us out of the control of the enemy so the enemy has no power over us unless we give him control. Anything that you fear has power over you; whatever gets your attention has power over you. It is your choice whether to give the enemy ANY GROUND. As long as you keep saying, "I can't, I can't," the further down you go. In and of ourselves, of course we can't; but we *can* do all things through total dependence on Jesus. Independently we are defeated—dependent on the Lord, we're victorious. "Greater is he that is in you than he that is in the world" (1 John 4:4 KJV). Praise God!

4

MATURITY
AND WORTHINESS

Have you ever seen a shepherd give birth to sheep? Ridiculous! Sheep beget sheep, then sheep bring other sheep to the shepherd. That's not only accurate animal husbandry, but good Bible teaching.

Paul instructed the Ephesians in chapter four that there is one body, one Spirit, one hope, one Lord, one faith, one baptism, one God and Father of all, and that the Holy Spirit is the one who brings us together into a bond of unity. He puts us together and makes us whole.

The apostle went on to say that Jesus led captivity captive and He gave gifted men to the body of Christ—the prophets, evangelists, pastors, teachers, and apostles. The intention was for the perfecting and full equipping of the saints, "that *they* should do the work of ministering toward building up Christ's body (the church)." It's not the pastor's job to build up the body by doing all the soul winning; it is the job of the members of the body. The pastor is to teach his flock, feed them, nurture them, and care for those who are brought in. God's purpose was that the church might "develop until we all attain oneness in the faith and in the comprehension of the full and accurate knowledge of the Son of God; that [we might arrive] at really mature manhood" (v. 13).

We are not left in doubt as to what maturity is: "The completeness of personality which is nothing less than the standard height of Christ's own perfection—the measure of the stature of the fullness of the Christ and the completeness found in Him" (Eph. 4:13). The fullness of Christ is a totally integrated person. It is a fullness of personality—the mind, the will, and the emotions in complete oneness. The Holy Spirit is to have master control so that the whole man is saying, "Yea, yea, yea," to God. Then a person is no longer fragmented. Jesus came to break down the middle walls of partition.

Some of us are so fragmented that our emotions are in one place, our minds in another, and our wills somewhere else and they don't agree. It is constant war. If you can't control your emotions, you block them off in a corner and your mind won't let you express them. The next thing you know, you've created a monster that you're afraid of. So you try to keep your emotions buried.

But Christ was a man completely at peace in every facet of His personality. He was fragmented in nothing. He was at home being emotional. He could cry; He could have compassion; He wasn't afraid to be tender. He was totally in touch with His emotions. He was in touch with His thinking and His feeling. That's what He wants for us—to be totally integrated so that the Spirit will have complete control over every area of our lives.

To be filled with the Spirit simply means to be controlled by the Holy Spirit. When our passions, our desires, our financial lives, our social lives, our academic lives—when everything is under the lordship of the Holy Spirit, we are not running here and there with upset feelings and emotions as situations come up. We don't complain, "I can't handle that." We *can* do *all* things, the Scripture says, through Christ Jesus who strengthens us.

"Yes, I can!" needs to be the triumphant shout of every believer. But you may still be saying, "Yes, I can," only with your mind and be cowering and frightened in your emotions: "Oh, I just know I'm going to fail." The enemy of your soul will know that you are not whole in your response. It all starts with choice. I must choose that everything will be brought into subjection to the lordship of Jesus.

So what is one of the first things Paul admonishes us to do if we are to grow up toward that maturity, toward full stature in Christ? We are taught, "Strip yourselves of your former nature—put off and discard your old unrenewed self—which characterized your previous manner of life and becomes corrupt through lusts and desires that spring from delusion" (Eph. 4:22). Through what faculty does delusion manifest itself? The mind—that is where the battlefield is. Whoever has control over your mind has control over you. That's very important to remember.

Paul said in Romans 6 that to whomever you yield your members, that is whose servant you are. If you yield your members to righteousness, you are the servant of righteousness. If you yield your members to unrighteousness, then you are slave to it. That's why he instructs us to strip ourselves of our old unrenewed selves. What does your former nature say? "It's natural for me to despair; I can't make it." You're always struggling to make it and you are afraid of defeat. That's a characteristic of the old nature.

You're just sure you can't find the answers; there's an emptiness, there's a longing, an inner churning within you. Well, Christ comes to fill that inner longing and inner churning. Every man wants to be and is intended to be in right relationship with his God. The only one who can bring us into that is the man, Jesus Christ—not things. You can have a lot of things and still feel empty. You can accomplish a lot of things, but if you don't have a right relationship with God, you are still restless. Only through Jesus can God put His Spirit within our spirits and bring us back into fellowship with himself.

You say, "I know I'm a new creature in Christ, but I feel so unworthy." That is GROUND for the enemy. You are fragmented and the enemy of your soul will keep plaguing you with your unworthiness until you get a new mind-set that says, "I'm worthy through the blood of Jesus. *Christ is in me* so my worthiness comes from Him."

I find this feeling of unworthiness among believers wherever I travel. At a seminar on healing and wholeness that I was conducting, a certain man expressed that he could not partake in the Communion although he loved Jesus. He would weep through it because the enemy had plagued him for thirty-one years that he was not worthy enough to partake of it. I explained that the very reason he *could* partake was the fact that Jesus died on the cross and shed His blood to give him worthiness. Well, God got the victory, and as we closed that service with the celebration of Communion, that man was the first to partake. Praise God!

It is a powerful word that Paul uses—"delusion." That means "not reality." It is a lie because Satan is the father of lies. He can't tell the truth and we can't expect him to. He will never bring you anything good. Delusion means that he is trying to counterfeit something that is real. If the enemy is so worried about something that he has to invent a lie about it, why should we not cross over and find out what the real thing is all about?

So many people get hung up on the possibility that the devil can counterfeit speaking in tongues. So what? Does that mean that God doesn't give the real thing?

5

REPROGRAMING THE COMPUTER

As long as you keep the old mind-set, you will never become a whole person. You have to put a new program into your "computer." If you have reprogramed the computer and try to feed the old program into it again, what does the computer do? It rejects it—*this does not compute; this does not compute*. And it goes on and on in a little monotone. If you get your spiritual computer reprogramed and the enemy comes along with a negative, all you have to say is: "This does not compute!" or "NO GROUND!" or "There is no vacancy here for that, because it has been filled. The ground where this was is occupied."

"Be *constantly* renewed in the spirit of your mind" (Eph. 4:23). How could you do that? By "having a fresh mental and spiritual attitude," having a new way of looking at things. If I stay down in that old rut of "I can't do it," the enemy will have a field day. There will be a war.

When we become new creatures in Christ Jesus, *all*

things become new. We have a whole new program. Everything about you—emotions, passions, and all—has changed. We spend so much time concentrating on the old that we never get acquainted with the new. You may not even know the new you. Jesus has to show you who you are now, because you still think about yourself in the same old way.

At one of our seminars, a young woman so easily and beautifully received the baptism in the Holy Spirit and with it the release of her prayer language. She was so excited. "I never heard me like this before!" she kept repeating. "I prayed a lot before, but I never heard me like this!" It was all new to her but the faculty to do it had been there all along. She had to get a new mind-set to reach out and believe that it was available, and that it was for her, then open up and release it and *act* like she could. In doing that and not saying, "I can't do it, I can't do it," she said instead, "Well, okay, I'll try," and she opened up her mouth and it naturally came out. I didn't even have a chance to pray for her! Something that was spoken triggered reality in her mind and suddenly everything in her agreed and consented to that. So there was no way that she could not. It is that simple. But not until she brought her emotions and her will and her mind *together* and said yes with wholeness could she have done so. She got past having doubts. She had her P.H.D!

When I was seeking to learn the Lord's voice, I came across this passage: "The sheep listen to his voice and heed it. . . . When he has brought his own sheep outside, he walks on before them, and the sheep follow him, because they know his voice. They will never . . . follow a stranger . . ." (John 10:3-5). A lot of you may have underlined that Scripture and thought how good it is. But did you ever get around to asking the Lord to teach you how to know His voice? When I read that, I prayed, "Lord, you said that your sheep know your voice. Well, I'm one of your sheep and I don't know your voice. Teach me to hear your voice."

And He said, "You listen and I'll teach you."

I had heard that passage of Scripture since I was a little girl but I had never done anything more than agree with it mentally. At this point it became a promise to me—"my sheep *know* my voice"—but I had never got around to really acting on that truth. It seems that we listen to anything. The enemy has a ball just filling us full of junk. But when we realize that we don't have to listen to anyone but the Lord, we tune in and listen for His voice. There's no reason for us to jump all over the place listening for something strange and wondering, "Is that you, Lord?"

Get to know His voice; that's how you recognize that it's the Lord. Spend time with Him. If you want to be intimate with someone, what do you do? You get into their presence; you start spending time with them; you start learning their ways; you want to know as much as you can about them. In the same way, the Scripture says, we will grow and mature as we come to know the full, accurate knowledge of the Son of God. There is no short cut to spending much time with Jesus.

When I found this passage I could have said, "Oh, well, that's a good Scripture; yeah, I'll underscore it and quote it around." Would that have helped me to know His voice?

No. But I had to say, "I *can* know your voice. You said so in your Word. I accept that. I *choose* to know your voice." Then I say, "Lord, make this real to me and put everything in alignment with the fact that I can know your voice." That brings an expectation. Then I move in to the place and get into the condition to hear and experience God talking to me.

Where would God talk to you? Where would Christ speak? Where would the Holy Spirit speak? In the air? No, *in you*. Right? And if you've brought all your faculties into subjection to Him, what would be the faculty He would use to communicate with you? Your mind. God will impregnate your mind with His thoughts. He said that He would write His laws in your heart and put His thoughts in your mind. If you are being renewed in the spirit of your mind and bringing your mind into subjection to Him, you don't have to fear the thoughts that come into your mind. How do I know this is God? How do I know this is not just my thoughts? You can check it out by God's Word.

Start out with basic truth. Where is Jesus? He is in me. This is the same pattern of relationship as between Jesus and His Father. The Father was in Jesus. "Believe Me that I am in the Father and the Father in Me" (John 14:11). Jesus never walked in a conscious state of separateness from the Father. As Christians, we still act in dichotomy: Jesus is here and we are over there. He has a mind and I have a mind. He has emotions and I have emotions and I have to go out of myself to find Him. Instead, we should realize that Jesus *has come in* and enhances everything that I am with himself.

We are told in Scripture to "Let this *mind be in you,*

which was also in Christ Jesus" (Phil. 2:5 KJV). He walked
in that oneness with the Father. Do I walk in a oneness of
mind with Him? Do I know that I am really one with
Jesus? If I know that, and there is only one mind between
us, can God not implant His thoughts within me? So why
should I have this battle whether what I hear is His voice
or just mine? Who am I? One with Him!

I can always check out what my thoughts are. "Lord, if
this is of you, I accept it; if this is not of you, the blood of
Jesus is against it; I don't want any part of this."

Here is another test: The Lord is never in a hurry.
Satan is in a hurry because his time is running out. He
likes to give us a push. Jesus quietly persists and His voice
doesn't fade away. The Holy Spirit gently nudges. And
the voice of God is consistent.

You can ask the Lord to reveal Scripture to back up
what you believe He is saying to you. But don't expect to
open the Bible and find, "Go to Cincinnati." You'll never
find, "Catch a certain train and go to Los Angeles on
February first." But you will find in Scripture that there
were similar specific situations where God spoke to the
minds of men in details. Scripture has principles that we
are expected to apply to practical needs for guidance. Paul
said he had dreams and visions. Most people are afraid of
putting any validity in their dreams. But God is not
limited. He still speaks however and whenever He wants
to. You can inquire of Him, "Lord, I had this dream. I
don't understand it. Is there something you want to say to
me?" Maybe there will be, and maybe not.

Paul said He perceived a man from Macedonia and
counted it as guidance to go there. He started out but was

led to stop by a lot of other places en route that undoubtedly God had planned for. I've heard ministers say that in our day God does not deal in specifics. But when I get into the Word of God, I find God doing just that. God will give you specific directions when you need them.

But you have to believe that God will talk in you. Who am I that God should talk to me? I'm His kid. I'm His child. Most fathers like to converse with their children—even if they have to call long distance. They get excited when the phone rings and it's Sally or John. They can't get to the phone fast enough.

Paul goes on to say we should have ". . . a fresh mental and spiritual attitude; And put on the new nature (the regenerate self) created in God's image, (Godlike) in true righteousness and holiness" (Eph. 4:23, 24). My new mind-set is that my very nature is holy. What did God say? "Ye shall therefore be holy for I am holy" (Lev. 11:44 KJV). He doesn't say to strive to be holy, to keep laws and traditions and doctrines to get holy, or to pray to get holy, or to work to get holy. He says, "You *shall be* holy."

If you read a Holy Bible, you will be filled with a Holy Spirit, right? And if you live in fellowship with a Holy God, what else can you be but holy? Don't be afraid of the word. "Me? I can't be holy!" That's the old mind-set. This holiness has nothing to do with a denomination but with a personal relationship to God. We must have a new mental attitude: "I'm somebody! I'm a child of the King! I'm no longer drooping. I'm a direct heir and descendant of God! Jesus is my elder Brother and God is my Daddy!" Then He puts within me His HOLY Spirit who keeps the connection open so that there's nothing that can stop me from touching home if I need to. I can follow the road map (the Bible) that tells me how to stay in touch. All the channels are open!

6

AND DEPROGRAMING

Since I know now *who* I am, the first thing I have to do is reject everything that is not like me or my heavenly Daddy or my elder Brother. That is deprograming.

Paul instructs us, "Rejecting all falsity and done now with it" (Eph. 4:25). Who is supposed to do the rejecting? *You.*

How can you know how to reject that which is false? God puts the Spirit of truth in you. He becomes resident within. He says that our spirits would bear witness with His Spirit whether a thing is of the Lord or not, whether or not it is truth. So if my spirit is not bearing witness, then the thing is false and I have the right to reject it. How do I reject it? By saying, "NO GROUND! I'm *not* going to take this into my mind or my emotions or my will."

Be careful now. When you reject it, don't keep the door open just a crack and say, "Well, maybe that might be a little right." That would get your attention and when it has your attention, that is GROUND for the enemy. He can start to move in.

When I first asked the Lord to teach me His voice, He began to tell me who He was. He said, "First, I'm sovereign." I like that word. He's the biggest—there's none bigger than He is. "I'm *It*." I AM is His name. Then He went on to say, "I'm all majesty; I'm all power." I got to thinking, yeah!

"Therefore, because I'm sovereign, I speak first," He said.

That's pretty good. Since He is sovereign and speaks first, you may find it is right to follow your first inclination. You can always check it out: "Lord, is this of you?" Then if it is not of His Spirit, it will bear witness with your spirit that it is not. Then it becomes a settled thing.

But some of us are so loyal to our concept of our church and we have so many hang-ups, traditions, dogmas, and prejudices, that our minds won't let us accept new things. Therefore we reject vital biblical truths. But the Word doesn't say to reject the *truth*, but to reject all *falsity*. Sorry to say, even some of us Christians have been programed incorrectly. A lot of what we have been taught and raised in has not been God's pure truth, even though we got it from the church. The hardest job that I had in my early spiritual growing experience was unlearning what I had learned. Much of it had nothing to do with my personal relationship with Jesus but with the dogmas of the church that I belonged to.

We have to put God's new ideas in the place of the old. "Reject all falsity and be done with it." Don't play with it—reject it and forget it. "God, you said it in your Word, I believe it in my heart, and that settles it in my mind." There should be no wavering.

Then Paul makes it very practical. He says that if you've ever lied, reject lying—you don't have to lie any more, you are to choose to tell the truth. In every situation, turn to Him. You don't have the same needs you had before; you told lies to be bigger than you were because you didn't have a very good image of yourself. But now you have the greatest image there is—you are made in the image and likeness of Jesus! You don't have to steal any more because you're not going to miss out on what is due you. Your everyday reactions are being transformed. Every time you read the Word, every time you come together with believers or listen to messages, God, by the Spirit, is changing you (2 Cor. 3:18). As you find the truth and consent to it, a process takes place and you are being reprogramed.

The Scripture tells us, "But whenever a person turns (in repentance) to the Lord, the veil is stripped off and taken away" (2 Cor. 3:16). What veil? The veil that had closed his mind to the realities of the Spirit is removed. "Now the Lord is the Spirit, and where the Spirit of the Lord is, there is liberty—emancipation from bondage, freedom" (v. 17). I was in bondage and you were in bondage to the negativity of life prior to knowing the Lord Jesus Christ. Jesus said, "If the Son liberates you—makes you free men—then you are really and unquestionably free" (John 8:36).

Free sometimes? On occasion? When you feel free? When you act like it? You mean *just plain free*, period? Do you *act* like you believe it? That's where the problem lies.

Paul said, "All of us, as with unveiled face, [because we] continued to behold [in the Word of God] as in a mirror the glory of the Lord, are constantly being transfigured into His very own image in ever increasing splendor and from one degree of glory to another. [For this comes] from the Lord [Who is] the Spirit" (2 Cor. 3:18). Not our working, not our laboring, but as we behold and get into fellowship with Him, we become reprogramed. I *can* become like Him.

According to Paul, "It is God Who is all the while effectually at work in you—energizing and creating in you the power and desire—both to will and to work for His good pleasure and satisfaction and delight" (Phil. 2:13). God so loved us that He didn't even leave us to muster up or conjure up a desire to do His will or to want to come for fellowship with Him. He implants in us the desire to become what He said we already are. Now *that's* a loving Father!

From the beginning our Father never wanted us to become slaves to our emotions and passions. His whole desire was that we should walk in constant communication with Him. But Adam, our forefather, chose to break that relationship, putting himself in ascendancy by believing a lie. That lie was appealing to his senses and he got snared. But we can come into complete relationship and wholeness of personality again by the constant renewing and reprograming of our minds. We choose, moment by moment, to be in complete alignment with the will of God.

We need to have one thing settled before we can move

into the reality that I'm trying to share: I can do nothing
without Jesus. Jesus said, "Apart from me . . . you can
do nothing" (John 15:5). Because anything that you think
you can do or anything that you attempt to do apart from
Jesus, is GROUND for the enemy to cause you defeat and
hassle you. That's the very opening that the enemy
wants. Settle it then: I can't do *anything* apart from
Jesus; but I can do *everything* through Him. You may feel,
"I can't face this situation; it's too big for me." Then say,
"Jesus, do it for me, through me, in me, and as me," and
then He alone will get the glory.

There is a story about a little boy who was trying to
move a heavy stone in his front yard. He was tugging
away at the stone, sweating and straining because the
stone was so much bigger than he was. It did not budge.
His father walked out and offered, "May I help you?"

The boy said, "Oh, no, daddy. I'm going to do this all by
myself." He kept struggling until his dad came back
again.

"May I help you?" Again the boy refused. The father
said, "Son, why don't you use everything you've got?"

"I am, dad; I'm trying but I can't move it!"

His dad said, "But you haven't asked *my* help."

The child had his father's strength fully at his disposal
but he was attempting to do the task on his own. "Without
me you can do *nothing*," Jesus said. That attitude needs to
become a basic part of our new mind-set program.

But the other side of it is, "I have strength for *all things*
in Christ Who empowers me—I am ready for anything
and equal to anything through Him Who infuses inner
strength into me, [that is, I am self-sufficient in Christ's

sufficiency] " (Phil. 4:13). I must choose to make Him Lord over every situation. These new programs have to become part of our practical, everyday experience.

If I don't know how to be a mother, I ask Jesus to teach me how to be a mother. If I don't know how to be a father, I ask Jesus to teach me how to be a father. I'm helpless apart from Jesus. He is my strength, my redemption, my patience. And if I want patience aside from Him, I want *self*-patience. I would be neglecting the reservoir of His patience in me. So, *off* with the old program and *on* with the new!

7

DEVELOPING *NOW* FAITH

The key to the NO GROUND walk is the power of the Holy Spirit. Through His enabling we can experience a new mind-set in our everyday living. As we surrender to the complete lordship of Jesus Christ, the Holy Spirit becomes the controlling factor to bring every area of our lives into perfect submission and wholeness.

It must be clear, however, that everyone who has received Jesus Christ as personal Savior *already has* the Holy Spirit residing in them. But whether or not the Holy Spirit is *in control* is determined by whether we are *filled* with the Holy Spirit. When we are born again, many of us unfortunately keep our hands on the controls of our lives and feed in the old programs. When we make the choice to receive the filling of the Spirit, or the baptism in the Holy Spirit or whatever terminology you use, then we give the controls over to Jesus Christ. The Spirit can then get on with the job of reconciling everything in our lives to God.

Some people have a problem with the concept of being

filled with the Holy Spirit. They wonder whether that means getting *more* of Him—whether they had a little at first, now more, and later still more. The Holy Spirit is a person. You either have Him or you don't. The only way you can receive more of the Holy Spirit is that you become more aware of Him, and you give Him more of the right of way in your life.

Don't ask for *more* of the Holy Spirit, ask for the *gift* of the Holy Spirit, and you will receive Him. Luke 11:13 does not mean that you will get more of Him in the sense of quantity when it says "how much more. . . ." There is a gospel song that I personally don't sing. The words are, "I want more of Jesus, More and more and more; I want more of Jesus than I ever had before." Jesus is a personality; you can't get any more of a person than his person. We are told that God does not give the Spirit "sparingly or by measure, but boundless is the gift God makes of His Spirit!" (John 3:34). He doesn't measure out how much He gives. He gives the Holy Spirit and that's it.

As I grow in my relationship with Him, I become more conscious of the Holy Spirit in my life. I become more sensitive to Him. It's not that I have any more of the Spirit than I had before. I just become more dependent upon Him and His power. That is what being filled with the Holy Spirit means—less of me filling the space in my life, and more room given to Him to occupy and control.

God is so gracious that He has given man free choice and will never violate that. It is up to us to choose whether to be obedient to the Spirit of God or not. We can choose God's highest and best or we can settle for second best. An incident in my own life brought that very clearly to me.

On one occasion when we were taping the PTL Club in Florida, the Spirit of God was moving in a fantastic way among the two thousand people there. The song, "It's Through the Blood" had just been sung and the second verse was, "I'm determined not to accept defeat." That had been the lesson God was teaching me for some time—to refuse to accept any form of negativity or defeat.

Well, I felt the anointing of the Lord upon me and I turned to Jim Bakker and said, "Jim, may I say something?"

He said, "Yes, Rev." And after I had expounded on the subject with all my heart I finished with the statement, "Before this body of people and every angel that's hovering over this place, I declare that I am determined *not to accept defeat!*"

Then the anointing of God came upon us so heavily that people began to cry. Jim got up and said, "I have to obey God, I have to obey God." He walked over to Nancy Harmon who is a vocalist with "The Victory Singers" on PTL-TV and told her that the Lord had laid on his heart to give her the PTL travel bus. Then he turned and said, "I'm not finished yet." The board had just bought Jim a new automobile and he said the Lord revealed to him that I needed a car and he gave *me* a brand new automobile—his own car!

I just sat and stared at him because I had just made a statement a couple of hours before that *that* kind of car wasn't *my* kind of a car. PTL had an $89,000 financial need at that time which had to be met by the next morning. Humanly speaking, the situation looked impossible. But God began to speak to the people about the need and in less than twenty minutes, without an offering even being taken, people just started walking up to the platform to give money toward the debt. Thirty-six thousand dollars was given at that meeting. In less than twenty-two hours the entire $89,000 need was met—for the praise of God!

But I was sitting there stunned because the kind of car Jim had given me was not my kind of thing. So I went back to my hotel room and prayed, "Lord, I have to be honest, (that's one of the things I learned early in my walk with the Lord—to be strictly honest with Him) and as much as I appreciate it, Lord, I just don't want it."

I knew exactly what that car would do—it would separate me from a lot of people. Some would get hung up about it, other people would get mad—the whole bit. "God," I said, "I don't want it, but I've been praying for your highest and best and if *this* is your highest and best for me, then I'm accepting this as a gift from you. I'll thank the individuals through whom it came, but I know the gift is coming from you."

That was an act of my will. I consented mentally but emotionally I did not accept that gift. I said, "All right, Lord, I've done this by choice; now it's up to you to bring my emotions up to the level of truth that has been revealed to me." I let it lay.

During the day, in my consciousness, it was fine; but as soon as I lay down to relax, the inward hassle started about the automobile. You see, I had not accepted it with my *whole* being. I admit it took me another week before I could accept it wholeheartedly, mentally, emotionally, and by an act of my will—and I haven't had any problems with it since. Everything else came into alignment with that. By myself, I didn't know how to bring the whole of me to accept that reality, but I asked Jesus to do it for me. And in doing it for me, He did it through me, in me, and He did it as me. On my part, when all kinds of negatives came flying into my head, I never handled them, I never reached up and grabbed them, entertained them or played with them. I insisted that they had NO GROUND in me!

So many times we get hung up and try to force ourselves to accept something—good or bad. But it is Jesus' responsibility to make it real to you, so relax and live and move by faith. *Faith* is the key.

So many people misquote Hebrews 11:1 by starting to quote with the word "faith," but that is not how it reads. The *first* word is the key word: *"Now* faith. . . ." That is *present* tense faith. We've had *past* faith for salvation, we have *future* faith for total redemption of our bodies, but what we need is moment by moment faith for the situation we are in *now.* The faith I had yesterday to lay hands on people for healing, to pray for needs, or whatever my situation was previously, is gone with yesterday. In what is my present faith? My faith is in the faithfulness of God.

I also discovered early that the enemy of your soul could come along and try to steal your faith if you don't develop it. Scripture says that every man is given a measure of faith but it's how you develop it that counts. Some people, even pastors, have said to me, "Oh, I've come to the conclusion that you are more spiritual than I am, Ev, or you have more faith than I have."

I answer, "No, I don't have any *more* faith than you; everyone has the same amount of faith; and I don't have any more of the Spirit of God than you have. I'm just a little more developed! I've used it. I've put into practice what I believe." If God has said it in His Word and Jesus has made it a reality in the example of His own life, then He tells me I should go ahead and do what He did and even greater works. If I don't start where I am, how can I grow?

I started out developing faith as a housewife, not in the ministry. I was just a simple gal who believed the Word of God. I'd be frying bacon and the bacon would pop up and I'd holler "Jesus!" and it wouldn't hurt and burn me. Or I'd be sewing for my children and run the sewing machine needle through my finger and would cry "Jesus!" and watch the blood come up and go back again without injury. I was developing my faith from little, everyday occurrences.

One day I was looking out the window and the window fell on my head. I went instantly blind. It was just as if I had been split in half—I couldn't hear out of one ear and I couldn't see. Just as this happened, the Spirit of God said, "Nine o'clock." Naturally, everyone wanted to rush me to the doctor. My children were all upset. I said, "I belong to Jesus and it's okay." I knew it within my innermost being. I could not see and hear but it was all right. I had faith and I had peace. At exactly nine o'clock that night, my ear popped open and my eyes could see again. I didn't understand why it had to be nine o'clock but I didn't have to. I just believed God.

The Scripture says, "Now faith is the *assurance*. . . ." That's another word I like—something that the body of Christ lacks. We have more *insurance* than we have *assurance.* "Now faith is the assurance (the confirmation, the title-deed) of the things[we] hope for, being the proof of things [we] do not see and the conviction of their reality."

We have such an assurance that the things we don't see are real, that we start acting like they are real. That's the kind of conviction Jesus gives. He said to the man with the withered hand, "What do you want?" Then He stood him right out in the middle of the crowd, not secretly, and looked around (Mark 3). "Now," He said, "stretch forth your hand." Jesus didn't see a withered hand, He saw the man's hand whole. His faith called the fact into existence. He had every conviction and assurance that when He asked the Father, He would do it. So He spoke the Word boldly.

To the disciples and to us Jesus declared, "Up to this time, you have not asked a[single] thing in My name . . . but now ask and keep on asking and you will receive" (John 16:24). The reason why you will receive is "so that your joy (gladness, delight) may be full and complete." It's the Father's good pleasure to give us the kingdom and He also delights to answer our prayers.

"Faith perceiving as real fact what is not revealed to the senses" (Heb. 11:1). Isn't that yummy? All truth is received in our spirits, not in our minds. Then it goes from the spirit to the mind and then out into actuality. There are a lot of things we believe in our hearts that our minds won't allow us to receive. We keep saying, "No, I have to see it, taste it, hear it, touch it, or smell it, and then I'll believe." But believing is what you do when you *can't* see. The world says, "Show me and then I'll believe." Jesus says, "Believe me and then I'll show you it was true."

Most of us live by faith every day and we don't realize it. How many people test chairs before they sit down? Do you test the car before you drive it or do you just get in and expect it to move when you turn the key? We get up every day of our lives by faith and have no guarantee that our legs will hold us when we put them on the floor. But we get up. There is no guarantee that you will see or be able to speak, but you wake up seeing and speaking. Praise God! You did it yesterday so it never entered your head that you couldn't do it today. *That's faith!*

We catch planes and go places by faith. I can't see my destination when I get on a plane but I strap myself in and the next thing I know I'm taking off. I hear a little "beep-beep" and a voice telling me what to do in emergency and what the weather is like and how many thousand feet high I'll be flying and the air speed. When the plane lands, I get out. Most of the time I never saw the guy who flew the plane. Maybe it was flying by remote control! But that didn't stop me from getting on.

8

LET'S TRY IT OUT

I realized one day that the enemy could try my faith to the point of totally robbing me of it.

I had a heart attack and ended up in an oxygen tent. I wasn't worried about dying; I wasn't worried about my children; the only thing I was concerned about was that I didn't want to lose my faith.

I said, "You know, Lord, how people can go all the way down to the wire and get scared and blow the whole thing. I don't want to do that and disgrace your name. I know the enemy can try to steal my faith, so I'll tell you right now what I'm going to do, God. I'm going to take this *little bit of faith* that I have and give it to you in exchange for your *faithfulness* to yourself. From this point on, you don't ever have to be faithful to Evelyn; just be faithful to yourself." I realized that Jesus was in me, and if He was faithful to himself, I would get the overflow! God said, "I am alert and active, watching over My Word to perform it" (Jer. 1:12).

I've seen so many healings take place where the symptoms apparently do not change immediately. Most people look at symptoms rather than dealing with the root of the thing. That's a false perspective. But God is the Great Physician who deals with the root of the problem.

For a headache, some people go to the medicine cabinet and get an aspirin. But they are just treating the symptom. The headache is only a symptom of a malfunction somewhere. It may break out somewhere else, then they have to do something else. But if they go to the Lord, they can get rid of the root of the problem! People think they are not healed because they still feel the same way. God didn't promise that you are going to *feel* any different; He said you would *be* different. That's something else.

But "faith perceives as a real fact what is not revealed to the senses." Most people naturally respond out of their senses; that's the result of Adam falling from his right relationship with God. He got locked into the sense realm. He became conscious of right and wrong, good and evil, and that became the law of his being.

But in Christ Jesus there is a new law that has for its standard, not right and wrong or good and evil, but "What is the will of my Father?" Even as born-again, Spirit-filled believers, in every situation the first thing we question is, "Is this right or wrong? Is this good or bad?" We don't bother to stop and find out *what is God's will* in this situation because we're so bound to the former attitude. Jesus never questioned whether something was right or wrong. He knew what it was. But He was possessed with the desire to do the will of His Father.

Let's Try It Out

Paul tells us that in the light of all that the Lord has done, we should make a decisive dedication of our bodies, presenting to Him all our members and faculties as a living sacrifice—not a dead one. "A living sacrifice, holy (devoted, consecrated) and well pleasing to God, which is your reasonable (rational, intelligent) service and spiritual worship" (Rom. 12:1). He says, "Do not be conformed to this world. . . . But be transformed (changed) by the [entire] renewal of your mind." How do we renew the mind? ". . . by its new ideals and its new attitude." That is a whole new program for our computers! What will happen? "So that you may prove [for yourselves] what is the good and acceptable and perfect will of God" (v. 2).

Every man can know the perfect will of God for his life if Jesus lives in him. When you say, "I can't know the will of God," you are GIVING GROUND to the enemy because the Word says that you *can* know. First of all, present yourself to God and then don't be conformed to this world (programed to it). The Word of God says, "For to us a child is born, to us a son is given; and the government shall be upon His shoulder . . ." (Isa. 9:6). If we have yielded our lives to Jesus, is the government *of our lives* on His shoulder? Do we take our value system from our divine source or is the world still regulating it?

The reason why so many of us don't know who we are or what we possess is because we are not well enough acquainted with God. "Acquaint *now* yourself with Him [agree with God and show yourself to be conformed to His will] and *be* at peace" (Job 22:21). Now that's a goody! First get to know God; second, agree with Him. How do you agree with God? Mentally, by an act of your will, which is choice, then emotionally, so that the whole of you is in agreement with Him. You have to agree with His Word in its entirety. God's Word doesn't have to make sense to you because it is operated by faith which goes beyond the sense realm. Faith does not question; it responds. Show that you know Him; show that you agree with Him. How? By acting like it. Then He says, "Be." How does one "be"? *Live*; just *live*. Isn't that simple?

Let's try it out. God, I accept your Word. In your Word you said that certain signs will accompany those who believe: In My name . . . they will lay their hands on the sick, and they *will get well*" (Mark 16:17, 18).

So if you are in agreement with that, what will you do to show that you agree with it? You'll act on it. When the enemy comes along and says, "Just who do you think you are? *You* can't lay hands on the sick," you'll be in trouble if you haven't settled something first. You have to *choose* to do it. I must make my choice, act like it, and then I'm just going to simply live and be at peace no matter how much the enemy hassles me.

I *can* do whatever He *said* I can do. Do you feel like you can do it? No, maybe not, but *He said* you could. Since He said it, He is responsible for doing it. How is He going to do it? Jesus himself is still laying hands on the sick, you know, but He is doing it *through you*.

How do you know this is for today? Because "Jesus Christ, the Messiah, [is always] the same, yesterday, today, [yes,] and forever—to the ages" (Heb. 13:8). The human body of Jesus Christ is sitting at the right hand of the Father, but He indwells us by His Spirit so that *we* become the visible body of Christ. Whatever is spoken in the Spirit, in order for it to be executed, has to be done through *our* hands, *our* eyes, *our* ears, *our* tongues, *our* feet. The Scripture says of Jesus, "God has prepared for me a body and I've come to do thy will, O God." Where else is He going to do the will of the Father but through me? That's how you can cancel out all the little thoughts that the enemy whispers to you when he tries to put you down. If you are settled in that, then he has NO GROUND.

Just go ahead and tell the devil who you are. Start out by saying, "I am—" As soon as you say that, do you know what you are declaring? You are in total identification with God, because that is what Jesus said: "*I am* the bread of life; *I am* the way, the truth and the life . . . ; *I am* the water of life; *I am, I am, I am.*" Where did He get that? From His Father.

In Exodus 3:14 God had given Moses directions to go down to tell Pharaoh to let His people go. Moses asked, "Who shall I tell them sent me?" You see, up to that time, all that the people knew was that He was the God of Abraham, the God of Isaac, and of Jacob. God said to Moses, "I AM WHO I AM and WHAT I AM and I WILL BE WHAT I WILL BE: and He said, you shall say this to the Israelites, I AM has sent me to you!"

In any given situation, I am going to be what I am going to be. I think the greatest thing we can ever do is *just be*. The world says "Do." Jesus says, "*You be* and I'll do." That will take the striving right out of your life and you will have pure rest. Just live in peace and take your cues from Him. Jesus is our example and He said that in thought, in word, in deed, in gesture, we're supposed to be exactly like Him—be conformed to His image and likeness. If we accept that as reality in our inward man, there *will* be an outward manifestation of it.

God will back us up just as He backed up Jesus. He's still the same! He's the same!

The world programs you to die. Jesus is reprograming you to live. Death could not keep Jesus bound to the grave. He was resurrected as victor for every man, woman, boy, and girl who has ever been born into the world. Paul, looking back on Jesus' victory, said, "O death, where is your victory? O death, where is your sting?" (1 Cor. 15:55). Jesus said, "I possess the keys of Death and Hades" (Rev. 1:18). When we receive Jesus Christ, what is the gift of God to us through Jesus Christ? Eternal life! From the moment we accepted Jesus Christ, we began to live in eternity—NOW!

Jesus said that there will be a generation that will never taste death. Perhaps we are that generation. When we get forty or fifty years old, we take it for granted that our knees are supposed to start creaking, and our eyes are supposed to start dimming and so we go along with that "natural" program. "I can't run like I used to; I can't do this or that. After all, I'm getting old." Or "I'm sixty and I've got to slow down." It is a mind-set because we've been programed that way. Why are we surprised if someone eighty-five years old can run eight or ten miles a day? My Bible says that Moses was 120 years old and his natural forces did not abate and his eyes did not grow dim. God said that He would renew our youth as the eagle's. But how many of us believe it? Do you think this is far out?

Let's Try It Out

These are some of the areas in which we GIVE GROUND to the enemy.

We are programed to concentrate on our limitations. But there are no limitations in Christ or in God. Why rely on ourselves more than on Him who is in us in power? Medical science says, "Well, that leg is broken and we've had to put all that steel in it and you'll never be able to walk." I know a great big man who is six feet, nine inches tall; he is walking around today without a limp even though his doctor had told him just that. But he forgot to believe it. And there was somebody who had enough faith in spite of what the doctor said to sign up that young man in advance to play basketball. And now he is playing for Jesus on God's ball team! What would have happened if that young fellow had agreed with the enemy and the world's diagnosis?

9

TESTED FOR STRENGTH

In all my family problems I determined to agree with God for all His promises to the point that I thought *nothing* could shake me: nothing in heaven, nothing on the earth, nothing under the earth, nor any spiritual power. After all, it was God who initiated His promises—I didn't think them up. On my part, I just opened myself to receive what He offered.

Boy, oh boy, did I ever get tested on *that*!

I have a son-in-law who was said to be a hopeless cripple in every sense of the word—not as much in his body as in his outlook and attitude. His mother hammered into him for years that he could never accomplish anything. Though he went to school and became one of the best dental technicians, he still had a "crippled" mind.

When he met me, I refused to treat him as a cripple. With all his skill, he was sucked under by his mind-set all his life because he had been programed that way. At one point he was ill in the hospital and the doctors were contemplating taking his leg off. I was believing and praying for him to be able to keep it. Every day the doctors came in to check it out and kept delaying the amputation. I could see that God was finally dealing with him.

I am only sharing this to show you how *not* to give the devil ANY GROUND with your children.

I didn't want my daughter to marry this man in the first place because she was a born-again believer and he was not. God said, "Let it alone, Evelyn." I couldn't reason with my daughter. God said, "Let it be. Do you trust me?"

I said, "Yes, Lord."

He said, "Then step back."

I delight in getting out of God's way and watching Him work. So they went on with the wedding. Hostility really began to build up because the young man was from a Catholic background and my daughter had to sign papers agreeing to raise any children in the Catholic faith and take instruction from the church. Every time I would begin to smart under it, God would remind me who He was and that He was in this situation.

The marriage went from bad to worse. My daughter would cry to me, "Momma, pray!"

But God would tell me, "Don't pray." Did you know that God will tell you not to pray about some things? That is why you should seek the mind of God carefully as to *whether* you should pray about something. I personally don't just pray for people because they ask me to; I pray when I have discerned the mind of God to pray. I believe that is scriptural because in the Old Testament a prophet was crying out to God and He said, "Don't pray for this people any more because I won't hear you." God said to me, "Evelyn, let it alone—don't pray. I made a promise to you; now you watch *me* do the work."

Well, my daughter had one child after another. It looked like about every eleven months she was having another baby. Every time I would go to talk to her, God would warn me to leave it alone. Then to make sure I wouldn't interfere with what He was doing, God put me constantly on the road in ministry. My daughter backslid spiritually and that wasn't easy to watch either. She was a gifted child, anointed of God to sing, but she was turning her back on God and refused to sing. I watched her go far afield with her husband.

I had taken care of my oldest grandson for two years and taught him the ways of the Lord. That little fellow at four years of age, literally with childlike faith, would pray and lay hands on people for healing. I watched him lay hands on a man who was six-feet-seven-and-a-half inches tall. When that big man sat down, his knees were as high as my little grandson. The man had problems with his knees and I could see my little grandson eyeing him. I knew he was going to do something but hung back because he was afraid. He finally came close to that big guy, looked up at him, quickly touched him on the knee saying, "Jesus, heal!" Then he jumped back because he was afraid of the man. God instantly healed the man through that little four-year-old's faith and prayer and he has never had a problem with his knees since.

Eventually, my daughter and her husband came and took this little fellow back and programed him with black superiority. They told him that everything I stood for was all wrong and turned him against "whitey."

I had a little granddaughter who apparently became instantly mute. Her mother got a call to come to the school, which was all black by their choice. The white teacher said, "I'm sorry, but we're going to have to put her back because she doesn't even know her name or where she lives or her telephone number."

My daughter looked at her and said, "You're crazy. She *does* know all those things and she can even spell."

This little five-year-old said to her mother, "I don't have to tell the teacher nothing. My daddy told me I never had to tell no white person nothing and no white person could tell me nothing." She had simply refused to talk or let anybody know what she knew.

I died. I just died. Do you understand that statement? But I refused to give the devil ANY GROUND. Whenever he came to hassle me about all the things that were going on in my family while I was out obeying the Lord to preach, I just said, "NO GROUND here. I'm God's property. He is in control no matter what."

My son-in-law began to shoot heroin. Through that terrible situation my daughter turned back to the Lord and got filled with the Holy Spirit and began serving in the church and singing again. And God has anointed her more greatly than before. But her married life was absolutely miserable. Finally the marriage broke up and she filed for a divorce. She said she had had it with him. When that happened, he stole her baby and wouldn't let her see him. After about six months, he finally brought the baby back and tried to harass her. The next day my son-in-law had a heart attack and was rushed to the hospital.

I watched all of this and I praised the Lord through it all, but God still didn't let me touch it. It was when I returned from a trip that I found out that the young man of only thirty was critically ill in the hospital.

He began to reach out to God in a way that he never had before. He called me on the phone and said, "Mom, I want to ask you to forgive me. In one of my rages, I picked up your picture and I broke it to pieces. When I stomped on that glass, do you know what? Something happened inside me. I don't know what it was, but I felt like everything went out of me and it scared me. I never felt so empty in all my life. All of a sudden I knew that I wasn't stomping you, I was stomping God. I had been rejecting the Lord and I really do need Him!"

He had started to seek God *without my saying a mumbling word*—nothing but the grace of God. I just held on in my heart with every atom and fiber of my being for those kids, asking God that my son-in-law might not be a cripple physically, mentally, or spiritually either. But even after that, God didn't let *me* minister to him; He sent other people into that hospital to minister to him—nurses, attendants, orderlies, and what not.

Do you understand what I'm saying? God told me not to worry about the terrible circumstances. I was just supposed to believe Him. God gave me the assurance that He was going to save. In fact, God promised me long ago that all three of my girls would live godly lives and they would be happy. I don't care at what stage they are now—the timing is up to the Lord—but God's promise *will* be fulfilled.

Each one of my daughters knows God promised me that because I told them. Whenever things get tough, do you know what they do? They phone me up anywhere in the world where I am and say, "Momma, things aren't going too good now, but I just tell God about it and remind Him of His promise to you." They believe it because I believe it and I act like I believe it.

Praise God, my son-in-law has now found the Lord, is in a church, and studying the Word. He is being reconciled to God in many of the desperately fragmented areas of his life. There is a lot of reprograming to be done, but he is finally putting himself under God's master control. Jesus never fails!

You will never hear Evelyn Carter say that to walk in the Spirit is *easy*. I say that it is *simple*. And there is a big difference. It takes every inch of your being to be simple enough to believe God. You must have an adult mind but childlike faith. You are not to be childish. Walking in the Spirit is the normal way God has planned for you so He did not make it complicated. Your tendency, when the enemy attacks those you love and who are close to you, usually will be to fight for them. But God requires you to surrender them to Him and in your giving, they are no longer yours but His. So He makes himself responsible for them.

I believe God is aware of everything that happens to us. Instead of seeing the *devil* in problem situations, I look beyond and see what *God* is doing, what He is saying, what He wants me to learn. I ask Him to control my actions and my reactions. I refuse to give ANY GROUND to the enemy of my soul.

Never, never, should we complain, "Oh, God, what have I done that you are punishing me through my children?" God is not vindictive. He's a loving Father. He doesn't lay sickness or troubles on anybody in order to punish them. He's not that kind of a God. Open yourself and listen to what He is teaching you through the problem.

10

EXPLORING OUR
GOLD MINE

Here's really good news for you: We know *who we are* in
Christ—now we're going to discover *what we possess!* It's
like going down into a mine and bringing up all the gold
bars that already have our names on them.

Do you know that you have an inheritance in Christ? Do
you want to find out what that inheritance is? I know who
can tell you—*Jesus Christ* is the *revealer* of our
inheritance. In Christ everything the Father has is ours.

But do you know what is *more* exciting than that? God
has an inheritance in *us!* Paul talks about "His glorious
inheritance in the saints" (Eph. 1:18). Have you ever
invited the Lord to claim His inheritance in you and use
His inheritance any way He sees fit?

It was mind-blowing to me when I discovered that God
had an inheritance in me. I realized that I had been so
busy trying to receive from God that I never gave Him an
opportunity to receive from me. He had put talents and
gifts in me that had not yet been revealed to my conscious

mind. From before the foundation of the world, God has purposed certain things in my life that I have never yet invited Him to claim. He has every right to use His inheritance any way He sees fit. It's amazing to me as I travel around to see that so many members of the body of Christ don't have that awareness. They are so busy trying to receive from God that they won't let God take from them.

One of the best ways to learn how *not* to give the enemy ANY GROUND is to find out what we have in Jesus. He has given us the perfect example. "Whoever says he abides in Him ought—as a personal debt—to walk and conduct himself in the same way in which He walked and conducted Himself" (1 John 2:6). Jesus was utterly dependent upon God. We are counterparts to Jesus as He was a counterpart in relationship to His Father. Jesus showed us how our relationship with God was supposed to be. In the world, we're taught to be independent. In Christ, we are taught to be totally dependent. Jesus said to us, "Apart from Me . . . you can do nothing" (John 15:5). No thing can you do apart and aside from Jesus. That needs to be a settled fact in the heart, mind, spirit, and emotions of the believer. If there is any doubt, we will always be striving to accomplish something on our own.

Jesus made a conscious choice. He was true God and true man but He chose to put His divinity into complete subjection to His humanity and never allow a thought or an action contrary or apart from His Father. He moved in a conscious state of total dependence upon God. So our highest goal should be to get to the place of being utterly dependent upon Jesus.

"Lord, I don't know how to walk—walk through me, Jesus; Lord, I don't know how to live—live through me, Jesus." Paul said that *whatever* we do in thought, word, or deed, we should do it as unto the Lord. Then who will people see? They will see our Christ.

What we are learning, if taken seriously, might be a little shocking, but hang in there—it will come out all right. We often need to have preconceived ideas shaken up in order to perceive what God is trying to reveal to us and through us in Jesus Christ. Do you know what the greatest sin is? Right away you might think about the so-called "big" sins like adultery, murder, or idolatry. But unbelief is the greatest sin. We have to believe God's Word in the mind, heart, spirit, and emotions so that there will be no unbelief whatsoever in us.

When I was young in the Lord, my church was saying that you *couldn't* do certain things in this age but my Word of God was saying that you *could* do them. I was struggling to believe the Word against what my pastor and everybody else was saying. The Bible claimed that we could lay hands on the sick and they would recover. One of the fantastic things about that passage is that it does *not* specify that the people to do this *must be Spirit-filled*. It just says that these signs will "follow them that *believe.*" Anyone who believes and will act like he believes is eligible.

I decided, "Well, I'm going to believe that." But then I said, "Lord, what if you don't do it?" I was just checking it out in case!

God said, "Well, if I *do* it, Evelyn, are *you* going to take the glory?"

77

I said, "Oh, no, Lord, the glory goes to *you*."

He said, "Well, if you aren't going to take the glory, don't handle the blame; just *do* it."

That freed me. I didn't have to worry or stick around to see if people were healed after I prayed. I could just lay hands on the sick, believe they were going to recover, and walk away from it. I didn't have to hang around for the results and plead, "O Lord, hurry up, please, come on, do it instantly, I want to see it!"

It's the world that says seeing is believing. But believing is what you do when you *can't* see. You just go and do it and if God doesn't back up His Word, it is *His* problem; it's not ours. The Bible says that God watches over His Word and He hastens to perform it. God's problem is that He can't find those who will perform so that He can perform. He wants to show himself to the world but He needs vessels who will believe Him beyond what they feel, what they understand, what they see, taste, touch, hear, or smell.

When God sent someone into the world to represent Him in His entirety, He sent Jesus for the pattern of how every born-again believer ought to walk. And we are debtors to do just that, because we have named the name of Jesus and accepted His shed blood as atonement for our sins. Don't get hung up to talk about *obligation* and being a debtor. The other side of it is that we have a *privilege* to let the world know that our Christ is a reality.

Jesus told us to take himself and the Father as a pattern. I pray "that they all may be one [just] as You, Father, are in Me and I in You" (John 17:21). And He said, "For their sake I sanctify myself." Why? So that we might experience the oneness that Jesus and the Father had. And then He said something great—that He was not praying for just those twelve men (in case we might feel left out) "but also for all those who will ever come to believe in Me *through their word* and teaching." Well, that included Evelyn—because when I heard Matthew, Mark, Luke, and John preach, it stirred my heart, so I know His promise is to *me*. Then Jesus said something else that is tremendous: "I do not ask that You will take them out of the world, but that You will keep and protect them from the evil [one]" (John 17:15). It's not up to you to grab up your skirt or hike up your pant legs and run away from the devil—it's God's responsibility to keep you from the evil one.

Why did Jesus ask the Father to leave us in the world? Because God needs witnesses. To what? To all that He is. If the world says, "Show me; I have to see in order to believe," what can God do? He has to raise up witnesses for the world to see. Where? In heaven where the world can't see them? In outer space where they can't relate to them? No. Right next door—in the same house—sometimes in the next bed. Sometimes in the *same* one! But He will raise up witnesses. God said, "*Be* a witness." He didn't say, "Struggle to *become* a witness." *Be* one.

If we get into the right relationship with Jesus Christ, as He had with the Father, then we'll walk like He walked, and we'll talk like He talked, and we'll act like He acted. How did Jesus come to this kind of reality? He made a choice that He would do nothing independent of the Father. He would let nothing originate in himself.

That should be our pattern.

I'm a person who needs to have somebody to depend on because in my early years, I didn't have anybody I could depend on. When I found out I could depend on the Creator of the universe—wow! The song, "Leaning on Jesus" has been the theme of my life. A minister once asked my oldest daughter, "Do you know what's wrong with your mother?"

"No," she replied (though I'm sure she could have itemized a lot of things!).

"Most people kinda lean over on the Lord, but your mother is falling all over Him."

That's total dependence.

Jesus said, "I assure you, most solemnly I tell you, the Son is able to do nothing from Himself—of His own accord; but He is able to do only what He sees the Father doing. For whatever the Father does is what the Son does in the same way" (John 5:19). Why couldn't Jesus do anything of His own accord? Because He had deliberately given the Father the right-of-way in His life and refused to do anything of His own free will. So right off the reel Jesus is saying, "I'm dependent. I can't do anything by myself." Jesus did what He saw the Father do—that's obedience. It never entered His head that He couldn't do it. If the Father did it, then He could do it because *they were one*. If we profess that Jesus Christ is our Lord and we are joint heirs with Him, whatever we see Him do, *we can do also*. When? Right now.

Someone said to me, "Oh, Evelyn, you don't really mean that's for us—that was only for Jesus. *I* can't see what the Father is doing." Let's dig out that piece of gold more carefully. . . .

11

PLUGGING INTO
THE TRUTH

Before we had all those fancy computers, the telephone company used to have an operator and switchboard. They still do in some small outfits. When you wanted to be connected with another person, or some source of information, the operator would plug you into the right socket.

God is our source of all knowledge, wisdom, and guidance. Jesus bought the right to the switchboard by His own precious blood and now we can have direct communication with the Father. Jesus said that the Holy Spirit is the revealer of all truth. When we are plugged into Him, when He dwells in us and fills us, we're on His permanent hot line.

Like Jesus, we *can* "see what the Father is doing" and, like Jesus, "whatever the Father does is what the Son does in the same way,"—and we can do it too. If you think this is not true, that GIVES GROUND to the enemy.

In John 16:13 Jesus said, "But when He, the Spirit of

Truth [the truthgiving Spirit] comes, He will guide you into all the truth—the whole, full truth. For He will not speak His own message—on His own authority—but He will tell whatever He hears [from the Father, He will give the message that has been given to Him] and He will announce and declare to you the things that are to come—that will happen in the future." The Holy Spirit will guide us into all truth, not partial truth. Three times Jesus said that the Spirit would reveal it to "you." I think that's so exciting. Whatever the Spirit hears from the Father, He will tell us! That includes even the things that will happen in the future. The work of the Holy Spirit is to reveal in the heart and mind and spirit of believers the perfect will of God. In any situation *you can know*, just like Jesus knew, what the will of God is for that situation. You can!

But the enemy says, "Who do you think you are?"

Then come back at him and *tell* him who you are!

Paul told us that we could know God's mind: "For who has known or understood the mind (the counsels and purposes) of the Lord . . . ? But we have the mind of Christ . . ." (1 Cor. 2:16). And, "Let this same attitude and purpose and [humble] mind be in you which was in Christ Jesus" (Phil. 2:5). In other words, let or permit the mind of Christ to work through the framework of your mind. Is it something you have to struggle for? No, it's something you have to allow to happen. People have questioned me, "You really think you're God, don't you?" No, but I have His Spirit! So have you.

The Bible says, "What eye has not seen, and ear has not heard, and has not entered into the heart of man, [all that,] God has prepared—made and keeps ready—for those who love Him" (1 Cor. 2:9). God keeps those things available for me because they are already mine. And not only does He do it for *me*, but for *you*.

"Yet to us God has unveiled and revealed them by and through His Spirit, for the (Holy) Spirit searches diligently, exploring and examining everything, even sounding the profound and bottomless things of God—the divine counsels and things hidden and beyond man's scrutiny" (1 Cor. 2:10). You have to go beyond the senses to find out the wonderful things of God. These things are revealed spirit to spirit.

Paul said, "For what person perceives (knows and understands) what passes through a man's thoughts except the man's own spirit within him? Just so no one discerns (comes to know and comprehend) the thoughts of God except the Spirit of God" (1 Cor. 2:11). Now *you* can start getting excited!

"Now we have not received the spirit (that belongs to) the world, but the (Holy) Spirit Who is from God, [given to us] that we might *realize* and *comprehend* and *appreciate* the gifts (of divine favor and blessing so freely and lavishly) bestowed on us by God" (1 Cor. 2:12). It is the Spirit who reveals it to us.

I like that word "lavish." You can just wallow in that. It means overabundant—kinda sloshy. Saying it in all reverence, I like to be a spiritual hog—I like to slop around in God's goodness! When I find one of the goodies that God has in the Word, first of all I claim it, then I just go to squealing and hollering, "Oh, God, I didn't know that was there!" And right away I have to use it, try it out to make sure it works. If you give a kid a toy, the first thing he does is play with it for a few minutes, then he starts taking it apart to see how it works. Well, I am truly like a child—a child of God.

A friend said, "If somebody says to you, 'that's a heart, Ev,' you say, 'Yes, I realize that is a heart, but I want to know how many parts it has and how many veins and arteries,' and the next thing you know, you've dissected it!" Well, I figure that if you know how something works, you can act like it and work with it. I think it is that simple.

Now Paul says, "And we are setting these truths forth in words not taught by human wisdom but taught by the (Holy) Spirit, combining and interpreting spiritual truths with spiritual language [to those who possess the (Holy) Spirit]" (1 Cor. 2:13).

And in verses 14 and 15, "But the natural, nonspiritual man does not accept or welcome or admit into his heart the gifts and teachings and revelations of the Spirit of God, for they are folly (meaningless nonsense) to him. . . . But the spiritual man tries all things—[that is,] he examines, investigates, inquires into, questions, and discerns all things." The spiritual man is *we* who are born of the Spirit.

So when you say, "I can't discern the Lord's will," that is not the truth because the Word says you *can*. But if we are enemy-taught, we will still keep saying, "Oh, I wish I knew the will of God; I want to learn the will of God; I'm striving to learn the will of God; I'm praying more, fasting more to find out the will of God."

The Bible doesn't say to fast for it; it says to *discern* it. We make such a job out of that which has already been freely given to us, because self and the world and the enemy say that you have to *work* for everything you get. But God says, "I *give* it to you by grace" (which means you don't deserve it, but you get it anyhow). It is like the little boy who runs in the house calling "Mommy, Mommy, I want a piece of bread," and when he gets it, it has butter and jelly on it! That's grace. All he asked for was bread. That extra is the dividend.

The spiritual man discerns all things "yet is himself to be put on trial and judged by no one.—He can read the meaning of everything" (1 Cor. 2:15). Is that your testimony? Can you read the meaning of everything? Why complain, "I just wish I knew the will of God. What's God saying to me through this or that situation? If I just had a little understanding." God says you *can* discern all things.

And if you really want your mind blown, read this: "But—you hold a sacred appointment, you have been given an unction—you have been anointed by the Holy One, and you all know [the Truth]" (1 John 2:20). Do you really believe that? The anointing is the Holy Spirit. *Through Him you know all things.* Why don't we act like it? Because we're fragmented. We believe it in our minds, theoretically, we've chosen to believe it, but emotionally we can't handle it. It's just too much. There's no way I can know everything. That would make me just like God. But who is *in* you? God! We don't have to strive to get the mind of Christ. The same Jesus who was with God the Father before the foundation of the world is now resident within the heart of the believer with all the knowledge that He ever had.

What do you possess? The totality of God. What is that?

Jesus, the Holy Spirit, the mind of Christ! But as long as your own mind is in gear, you block out the Holy Spirit's revelation. As you quiet yourself and move into the center, the core of your being, what happens? The knowledge of Christ flows into your mind. God said that He would write His love in our hearts and on our minds. Why then do we spend so much time doubting whether what is in our minds is of ourselves or whether it is of God? Jesus would not have stood around wondering that. He had made an irrevocable choice that He would never allow anything to originate from himself but always from the Father. Therefore, He never had to doubt what He received.

This passage says that you and I have become the receptacles that hold the thoughts, the feelings, and the purposes of God! How then can you think that you are a nobody? Why do you walk around thinking, Woe is me!, sitting half-dead, when you have all the thoughts, all the feelings, and all the purposes of God within you? The will of God is made manifest through us. That's really yummy! But the enemy of our souls doesn't want us to know this. He wants us to keep struggling to attain, struggling to grab ahold. Scripture says, "We have . . . and do hold. . . ." We think we have to work more in order to receive it. Wrong. If you come to this kind of reality, you can't help but walk and do the things that you're supposed to do.

Jesus never labored to heal the sick. He didn't pray in order to get the power to heal. He met a funeral procession on the street one day on the way to the graveyard. You have to know about Israel to know what a fuss people make about funerals with a whole string of paid mourners following along and wailing. Here was this great hullabaloo coming down the street. And the mother was weeping—it was her only child who had died. Jesus didn't stand there and say, "Lord, should I raise this man or not? I wonder what this mother will do? Will the Sanhedrin approve? Will the elders put me out of the synagogue?" Jesus had compassion for the woman and without any to-do He went up to the coffin and said, "Get up!"

The disciples must have thought, whatever is He going to do now? Jesus didn't pray a long prayer.

We seem to think we have to get ourselves in condition. We have to get up early in the morning if we are going to pray for the sick and we pray and fast all day and everything else so that our spirituality can be right on center. Then we go in fear and trembling, working ourselves up by praying, "Come on, Jesus," (just in case He doesn't want to come!) and then finally we pray, "Father, if it be thy holy and righteous will. . . ." And then, "Please, Jesus, heal, please!"

But Jesus just walked up to the dead man and said, "Get up" and the man got up.

We are totally helpless apart from Jesus, of course. But when we have received the resurrected Jesus Christ, full of power, into our hearts, did He throw that power away somewhere down the line and come into us emptied of His power? That's a lie from the enemy. Jesus promised us that greater works than He did shall we do. Why? Because He was going to His Father.

After Jesus said that He could do nothing by himself

and of His own accord, He then declared, *"The Son is able to do only what He sees the Father doing."* He never said, "I'm not able," or "I want to be able," He said, "I'm *able* to do whatever I see my Father do." Scripture says that the Father dearly loved the Son and disclosed to Him everything that He himself did (John 5:20). God showed His Son all His secrets.

Now it really takes an intimate relationship to share your secrets with someone. And Jesus loves *us* so much that He delights in sharing *with us* the things that are hidden. Jesus has given us the Spirit who is the revelator and delights in revealing hidden things to His own (John 16:13-15). He said that He didn't want us to be ignorant, so He whispers secrets into the innermost parts of our hearts.

Why should we ever doubt, "I don't know if that's God or if that's me"? We start checking it out with other people. "Do you really believe God would say . . . ?"

"No, I don't believe God would say . . ." answers someone.

"Me either. I sort of thought it was just me."

But His Word has declared, *"He will reveal. . . ."*

Unless we are determined to give NO GROUND to the enemy and let Jesus be Lord and then develop that intimate relationship with Him, we'll always be like seesaws in our thinking. But when we enter into a close relationship and get acquainted with a person, *nobody* has to tell us what that person would do. You know him so well. He is predictable. If we spend time with Jesus, we'll know His nature. When the enemy sows seeds of doubt in us, we should immediately shout, "NO GROUND! I know in whom I have believed and I am persuaded. I know Him so well that I know everything He will do."

That's the kind of assurance the Hebrew boys had as recorded in the third chapter of Daniel because they knew their God. When Nebuchadnezzar sent out the decree that everybody had to bow to the golden image he made, God's boys knew they weren't supposed to and refused because that was not God's predictable will.

The king said to them, "Who is that god who can deliver you out of my hands?"

They said, "Whether He will or whether He won't, that's His problem; as for us, we ain't bowin'!"

It was just that simple. God wouldn't have wanted them to bow. And they stoked the fire up seven times hotter than usual. It was so hot it burned up the ones who threw them into the furnace. And it burned up the ropes with which they were bound. When the king came down later and went peeping in, there were the Hebrew boys walking around.

And he jumped up and said, "I thought I put in three but I see four and they are not hurt!"

They said, "Oh, come on, what's the other one look like?"

And Nebuchadnezzar said, "He looks like a son of the gods."

Do you see that the intimate relationship of those Hebrew boys with God caused them not to doubt God regardless of the circumstances? They knew God could handle it. And He did. He sent in the first spiritual air-conditioning system and cooled the flames while the boys were still running around in them! Faith will do that for you. Everyone wants to be delivered *out* and God says that He will deliver you *in the midst*.

David knew about that too. He said, "You prepare a table before me." In a hidden corner where my enemies can't see it? No. "In the presence of my enemies" (Ps. 23).

In John 5:30 Jesus repeated that He could do nothing on His own but got His orders right from God. That was moment by moment dependence—a direct hot line. "Even as I hear, I judge and My judgment is right because I do not seek or consult My own will." If Jesus came to the conclusion that He had to have that kind of close relationship and identification with His Father, how do we figure we can do the things of Christ without that same total dependent relationship with Jesus?

I must make the decision that I can do nothing by myself. I can't even consult my own will; I have no desire to do what is pleasing to myself. That's a hard word. But if we take *any other route*, we give the enemy GROUND and he can get a foothold in our lives.

12

THE DIVINE UMPIRE

To prevent the enemy from having ANY GROUND in our lives, there are two things the Scripture says we are to let happen: *To let* the Word of God dwell in us richly, and *to let* the peace of God rule our hearts. Let's explore Colossians 3:15-17.

Verse 16: "*Let* the word [spoken by] the Christ, the Messiah, have its home (in your hearts and minds) and dwell in you in [all its] richness, as you teach and admonish and train one another in all insight and intelligence and wisdom [in spiritual things, and sing] psalms and hymns and spiritual songs, making melody to God with [His] grace in your hearts."

Verse 15: "And *let* the peace (soul harmony which comes) from the Christ rule (act as umpire continually) in your hearts—deciding and settling with finality all questions that arise in your minds—[in that peaceful state] to which [as members of Christ's] one body you were also called [to live]. And be thankful—appreciative, giving praise to God always."

A third very powerful passage follows in verse 17: "And whatever you do—no matter what it is—in word or deed, do everything in the name of the Lord Jesus and in [dependence upon] His Person, giving praise to God the Father through Him."

Do you know what was the first recorded oral Word of God in Genesis? "Let"—allow, permit, cause to happen. It is not, however, a passive word. How can you "let" peace? Because you already have peace, received from Christ when you were born again. "Peace I leave with you; My [own] peace I now give and bequeath to you. Not as the world gives do I give to you. *Do not let* your heart be troubled" (John 14:27). Don't permit or GIVE ANY GROUND in the area of allowing your heart to be troubled. Why? Because Jesus has given us His peace. Just let it out. Who can take His peace away from you? No circumstance—nothing—can remove the peace of God because the Holy Spirit sheds that peace abroad in our hearts. He puts it there as a permanent gift to believers. Nothing can nullify the peace of God.

So God says, *"You* let it operate." How can I make the peace of God operate? Situations come into my life where the most natural thing in the world would be to panic. How can I let peace abide? By refusing to GIVE GROUND to panic; by taking God at His Word.

What is that peace from Christ supposed to do? Rule in my heart. I am to let Christ be the law and the life of God resident within me because He is that already. I can refuse to get upset.

When we take away the basis or root of a situation, then there is no need to react to it. If I have peace, and peace is a gift, then anxiety and the disposition that is in me that would ordinarily cause me to panic has been taken away. I now have something to rely on. I know who I am in my relationship with God, so I am responsible for acting like it. God has put His peace within our hearts so that it will be a witness to ourselves and to others that we are children of God. God tells us that His peace should have the preeminence and be the ruler over all our affairs and act as an umpire. So what if there are storm clouds? Jesus is the One who says, "Peace, be still." He rules the wind and the waves.

Our hearts can say with the songwriter: "When peace like a river attendeth my way, When sorrows like sea billows roll, Whatever my lot, Thou has taught me to say: It is well, it is well with my soul."

Romans 8:28 declares that "all things work together and are [fitting into a plan] for good to those who love God and are called according to [His] design and purpose." That's for us. We love Him and are called according to His purpose. Regardless of what comes into our lives, it's working together for good. Instead of saying that the enemy is doing this or that, look beyond the enemy and give the credit to God. Say rather that the Lord is teaching you and helping you to grow. You would never know how much you have grown had you not entered into some difficult circumstances. It is in those times that you find out what you really believe.

After having taught and preached for many years, I went through a period of testing which revealed how much I believed what I believed. Not really how much belief I had, but how much of it had me. In one incident, I literally tried to panic and get upset because it looked like I should, but I couldn't. "When the enemy shall come in like a flood, the Spirit of the Lord will lift up a standard against him and put him to flight" (Isa. 59:19).

Until the situation gets tough, we don't know some of the things we have become immune to as we have started to learn to walk in the Spirit. Sometimes the enemy comes along and says, "If you really cared, if you really had compassion, you would react to this situation." We may not realize that it is the Lord who has stilled our hearts so that we don't get caught up in potentially upsetting circumstances and blow it.

We just GIVE GROUND to the enemy when we say, "Yeah, maybe I ought to act like I have more compassion and be affected."

Peace is the umpire that will continually be in our hearts deciding and settling with finality all the questions that enter our minds. One of the reasons why the enemy has such a field day with us is because we don't have things settled by our "divine Umpire."

When we read the Word of God and find a promise and claim that promise, then we ought to stand on that promise regardless of the circumstances. God says we should be "rooted and grounded." Where? In the Word. "God, you said it in your Word; I believe it in my heart; that settles it in my mind whether I feel like it, whether I see it, can taste it, touch it, or smell it. Lord, you said it and that's it!" Our Umpire's word is final!

Once you have settled a thing, you can forget about it and the enemy has NO GROUND!

13

CHANGING MY CLASSIFICATION

Many Christians don't know that their classification before God has changed. That gives MUCH GROUND to the enemy of our souls. Our classification is no longer *sinners* but has changed to *saints* and *sons*.

Let's get this straight and square with the Word of God. It is *not* true that saints *don't* sin. The point is that God has changed your classification and you are no longer a sinner. You are a joint heir with Christ. Therefore you can't approach God as a sinner the way you did before. You can approach Him as His child who has done wrong, but you can't deny your birthright. Your birthright is that you have been born anew into the family of God. How can you go back to calling yourself a sinner?

There is sin which means the "sin principle." Then there are *sins* which are deeds or acts. What happens when we are born again is that sin as a disposition or a principle, which had ruled our lives previously, has been totally erased and we've been released by the blood of Jesus. But *sins* as deeds or acts that we do, are what we confess moment by moment and day by day in order to keep in perfect fellowship with God and from which He keeps cleansing us.

By the Spirit of God, our nature has been changed from that old nature to the new nature which is in Christ Jesus. The nature of Christ has no desire to sin and that is our new nature. It becomes the ruling part of our lives and brings our minds, our hearts, our spirits, and our emotions into subjection to His lordship. Any desire in our being to practice sin in an out and out, premeditated way is removed.

John says that "no one who abides in Him . . . (deliberately and knowingly) habitually commits (practices) sin" (1 John 3:6). Why? Because the divine life remains within him and he has no desire to sin. He says that if anyone says that they haven't sinned, they are lying. That's why it's terribly hard for some people who have been raised in a church and have never gone far afield, who have been basically good people, to realize that they are sinners. They have never done any of the so-called "big" sins. But God said we've *all* sinned and come short (Rom. 3:23), because we were born with the *sin principle*.

When we become conscious of the fact that sin has separated us from God, then we cry out, and realize our need of a Savior. We receive Jesus as Lord, and the inborn desire to sin is gone. That's what makes us sons of God. Therefore, when you become a son of God, you should no longer approach God as a sinner but as a saint.

Basically, Jesus Christ didn't teach on sin; He taught on

relationships. The church teaches on sin and is constantly reminding us that we are sinners. The Spirit of God is the convictor of sin, but Christ comes to develop our relationship with the Father. As long as you don't have the sin question settled in your heart and mind, how are you going to develop a relationship with somebody whom you are afraid of or separated from because of the sins in your life? You will never draw near to Him.

When we draw near Him as our older brother and as a friend and lover, He knows what we are, and we know what we are, so we can enter into an open relationship with him.

We've been taught in the world that we should keep everybody at arm's length. There are few people whom we trust. We unconsciously carry over that attitude of distrust to our relationship with Jesus. We don't seem to realize that He knows all there is to know about us and *still* loves us.

During my prayer time I just like to sit and muse on the things of God and let the Holy Spirit bring passages of Scripture to me. When I was a young woman, I just loved the Lord so much; I wanted more and more of everything spiritual. Every time something was going on at the church, I would be there. I was so hungry for God. My pastor said to me, "You know, daughter, you're nothing but a spiritual hog. You just eat up everything you can find." So I learned early how to wallow in the Word of God.

There are times when I have tremendous yearning just to sit down and taste the Word. The Scripture says, "Taste and see that the Lord is good" (Ps. 34:8).

Sometimes when I am speaking to a group, the Word tastes so good that I have to stop and say "M-m-m-m-m!" because I want to savor it.

I heard the Lord speak to me one day during that kind of meditating time. He said, "Evelyn, do you know what is one of the biggest spirits among the body of Christ?"

"No, but I want to know because I'm 'nebby.' " That's a northern term and you may not know what it means. "Nebby" is curious. The old folks used to say, "Girl, you're so nebby. You're always poking your nose into something."

And He said, "The gluttony of overcompensation."

I said, "What?" I had never heard that—"the gluttony of overcompensation." Sounded tremendous! I knew God meant for me to dig in—to really spread out and explore. I knew I was getting ready to get a real goody so I got pencil, pad, and Bible and sat down. That's when the Lord said, "Let's reason together."

I said, "All right, Lord, what are you saying?"

He said, "Everybody wants to compensate and there's a lust for overcompensation. If people are little, or feel inferior, what do they do? They overcompensate for their feelings of inferiority by having everything big because they don't want to deal with the fact that they're little. They don't want to accept their own stature." God continued, "I made them that way. But rather than accept whatever their condition is, they will try to cover it up.

"Look at my people. Some of them are running around with a put-on grin on their faces while their hearts are breaking and they are crying inside; but they don't want anybody to come close. You know that the world plays games, but look at the shams my people have. If someone asks, 'How do you feel?' they answer, 'Oh, I feel fine!' And their hearts are breaking. But they don't want to allow anyone to enter in. Not only do they not want their fellow-men to enter in, but they won't even allow me to get into their inner hearts. They'd rather overcompensate, and live their lives without me rather than to be honest with me and expose their hurts for me to heal."

How true this is in the body of Christ! As a Christian, I'm always supposed to be on top of it, never in the valley. But, you know, I serve a God who is a God of the mountain *and* a God of the valley. If there are valleys, I don't have to go through them alone because when I get into the valley, He's there. How do I know? Because He is *in* me. And He is still in control of every situation. So I can say to Him while I'm in that valley, "Hey God, here I am down here in case you don't know it and I'm hurting." I like to punch in every once in a while and let Him know where I am!

He says, "Yeah, Ev, I know."

I say, "What are you going to do about it?"

He says, "Just waiting on you to ask."

But we figure that because we are Christians we are supposed to work everything out for ourselves. We misinterpret that passage of Scripture that says "work out your own salvation with reverence and trembling" (Phil. 2:12). The only thing that you work out is what He works in. If you don't allow Him to work in anything, you can't work out anything. That doesn't mean that you have to prove to everybody that you're saved. You let salvation become so much a part of you that it can't help but be manifested to everyone you meet. Then God puts you through circumstances and situations so that your salvation becomes a reality to you.

When we learn new truths, we can expect to find that God will test us to prove whether we know what we know. It is our opportunity to stand. Whatever place in your nature or disposition is a weakness to you, if you don't offer it to Jesus, it becomes GROUND for the enemy to plague you. He knows where you are weak.

Jesus said through Paul that when you're weak in human strength, then you are truly strong, able, and powerful in divine strength (2 Cor. 12:10). He never admonished us to be strong in ourselves, but only in Him. Paul tells us, "In conclusion, be strong in the Lord—be empowered through your union with Him; draw your strength from Him—that strength which His[boundless] might provides" (Eph. 6:10). You can overcome all things through Him, and you don't have to fear your own weakness. That's why He said that we should hunger and thirst for righteousness, "for they *shall* be completely satisfied" (Matt. 5:6). We need to get the Word of God into us to the point that it will settle every question that arises in our hearts and in our minds. God's Word is the last word on the subject—not what I *feel*; not what I *think*; not what I *desire*, or even *hope* for. But whatever God has said in His Word.

14

MORE THINGS TO SETTLE

Another fantastic truth is found in Romans 8:3: "For God has done what the Law could not do, [its power] being weakened by the flesh [that is, the entire nature of man without the Holy Spirit]."

Since this is true, can anyone who has named the name of Jesus say that he has a nature without the Holy Spirit? According to this passage, you cannot be a born-again believer and have a nature without the Holy Spirit.

Verse 3 continues, "Sending His own Son in the guise of sinful flesh and as an offering for sin, [God] condemned sin in the flesh—subdued, overcame, deprived it of its power [over all who accept that sacrifice]." We accepted the sacrifice when we received Jesus Christ. At the same time, we received the Spirit of Christ and He became resident within our nature. Can you separate Jesus from the Holy Spirit and from God the Father? You cannot!

Note this carefully: This does not say that one is *filled* with the Holy Spirit. It says that we *have* the Holy Spirit because he that is joined unto the Lord is one spirit (1 Cor. 6:17). If you have a spirit beside the Holy Spirit, then you have more than one spirit. That cannot be true. This is the kind of basic thing that you need to have settled. If not, then your confusion can grow because that area is still GROUND for the enemy.

If you think you have two natures, believe me, you are in trouble. The Word of God says that Jesus Christ took our old human nature and nailed it to the cross (Rom. 6:6). He put His own nature *in place* of that old human nature. The nature of God is now resident within you, and you *can't* have two natures.

What does this have to do with the enemy trying to get GROUND in us? *The enemy can't possess us,* but he can jab away at us, trying to get our attention, trying to make us believe that he is in us; but he is shooting at us from the *outside*. Something has to be on the *inside* in order for it to have control. Hallelujah!

Look at this Scripture. "Giving thanks to the Father, Who has qualified and made us fit to share the portion which is the inheritance of the saints (God's holy people) in The Light. [The Father] has delivered and drawn us to Himself out of the control and the dominion of darkness and has transferred us into the kingdom of the Son of His love, In Whom we have our redemption through His blood, [which means] the forgiveness of our sins" (Col. 1:12-14).

If I have been delivered out of the control of the enemy and I am in Jesus, that means that the enemy has no power over me whatsoever—NO GROUND. The only thing he can do is stand outside and throw dirt and darts at me and taunt me. *But he can't come in.* Why? Because he doesn't have any power over me. That needs to be a glorious, settled fact in the hearts and minds of believers. Praise God, the battle is from without, not from within!

The enemy also tries to GAIN GROUND in us by hassling us with condemnation, guilt, and blame. "Therefore [there is] now no condemnation for those who are in Christ Jesus" (Rom. 8:1). *Now* is present tense. Many saints don't know that. My version of Romans 8:31 is: "God bein' for me, who's got the audacity to be agin' me?" I didn't say they wouldn't be, but they have a whole lot of nerve, because if they're agin' me, they're agin' God. How can they say they love God and be against me? Because He and I are one. If all the saints understood that, they wouldn't have that old hangdog look. They'd stand up and be somebody!

Now don't get me wrong—I do not mean that no one can criticize me. You might walk up to me with a very constructive criticism. And I must listen to you as my sister or brother. But instead of allowing that criticism to hurt me, or to take it as a sense of personal rejection, or as a put-down, I should say, "Lord Jesus, I heard my sister or my brother. Now I lift this up to you to show me the truth."

It's not that you are not telling me the truth, but whenever I react and realize that I have hurt feelings, that's when I say to Jesus, "Lord, you had better cook me some more because I realize I'm not well-done in that area yet."

If you stick a fork into something that's done, it never resists. If I find myself resisting, I know that I'm not done, and I need some more work in that particular part of my life. I can't do anything on my own to correct that, so I pray, "Jesus, I want to expose this to you. I need your help."

Paul says, "But (as for me personally) it matters very little to me that I should be put on trial by you [on this point], and that you or any other human tribunal should investigate and question and cross-question me. I do not even put myself on trial and judge myself " (1 Cor. 4:3). When I read that, I almost jumped out of my skin! I thought, There's a man after my own heart! He even added, "And I *feel* blameless."

The Scripture says that Jesus Christ brings us to the Father faultless, guiltless, blameless, and sinless. That's how we are presented moment by moment before the Father. That's why Paul says, "I am not conscious of anything against myself, and I feel blameless" (1 Cor. 4:4). Because he took the Word of God at face value, God verified that he was blameless.

He said, "But I am not vindicated and acquitted before God on that account, but I tell you what—I don't judge myself because it's God's business to judge me; and until God tells me something is wrong with me, I ain't takin' it from nobody else, because it's God who does the judging."

It is the trick of the enemy of our souls to condemn. But there is therefore *now no condemnation*—right *now*—to them that are in Christ Jesus. I'm in Jesus; I'm wrapped up in Jesus. I don't have any desire to get out. I'm hanging in here by the blood of Jesus, so how can I be conscious of anything wrong with me unless my heavenly Daddy tells me there's something wrong with me?

If I had done something wrong when I walked through the door on the way to the platform to give a message, I would say, "Lord, I'm sorry."

He'd say, "Okay, Ev, that's all right." I would then stand before Him and before the audience just as clean and holy and righteous as if I had never done it.

I'm not going to listen to the condemnation of the person who saw me do what I did at the door. That's his problem if he judges me because God forgave me as soon as I uttered in my heart, "God, forgive me."

The Word says, "For the Lord sees not as man sees; for man looks on the outward appearance, but the Lord looks on the heart" (1 Sam. 16:7). We need to know how God feels about us in our hearts. Until my Daddy tells me there is something wrong with me, I'm going to act like there isn't anything wrong with me. I'm taking God at His Word and applying it to my life. I'm acting and living out my faith because "the just shall live by faith" (Heb. 10:38).

Somebody may come along and say, "Who does she think she is?" That gives me an opportunity to tell him. You overcome by the blood of the Lamb and by the *confession* of your mouth (Rev. 12:11).

There is no sense in singing "There is power, there is power in the blood" if you don't believe that the blood does what it does. If you keep feeling that you're still a sinner, don't sing that. You don't really know what the blood is all about.

Scripture says, "Without the shedding of blood there is neither release from sin and its guilt nor the remission of the due and merited punishment for sins" (Heb. 9:22). "And their sins and their lawbreakings I will remember no more" (Heb. 10:17). Now that's enough to make you do a jig! Then he goes on to say, "Now where there is absolute remission—forgiveness and cancellation of the penalty—of these [sins and lawbreakings] there is no longer any offering made to atone for sin."

He continues, "Therefore, brethren, since we have *full* freedom and confidence to enter into the [Holy of] Holies [by the power and virtue] in the blood of Jesus." It is not on my own merit, but because of His willingness to die for me that I can enter into the secret place with God—I can even *run* into the Holy of Holies. There's nothing to keep me out of the heart and presence of God. Why? Because Jesus has made the way.

I paraphrase the next verse to say, "By this fresh and new and living way which He opened for me through the separating of the veil of the Holy of Holies, His flesh, can we all come in with unqualified assurance." I don't have to qualify. I don't have to measure up. My heart is sprinkled and purified from a guilty conscience.

That's one of the problems in the body of Christ. Believers still hang on to their guilty consciences because they've never become *naked* before the Lord, and allowed the Lord to cleanse their consciences with the blood of Jesus. They accept forgiveness with their minds, and they accept it with their wills, but emotionally they are still trying to hide for fear they might be seen as they really are. They don't realize it is impossible to hide (Heb. 4:2).

My conscience needs to be cleansed because I am a new creature in Christ Jesus. I'm brand new. When people bring up what I did twenty years ago, I say, "Oh, that girl you're talking about died." That's scriptural. She did. She died in Christ. Why do I have to worry or feel guilty over something that a dead person did years ago?

Guilt is fear of being punished. But Jesus already took the guilt on himself so I don't have to worry about paying the bill for my wrong deeds. He stamped it: "Paid in full" and said, "Now you go ahead and live, Ev." It's that simple.

I want to tell you how to work out the nitty-gritty of giving NO GROUND to the enemy in this matter of guilt. I have a daughter over thirty years old who was conceived in sin. I had her before I got married. I was sixteen plus one month and fourteen days when she was born because I had cried out to God that I didn't want to have a baby when I was fifteen years old. I had that baby while I was looking for love. My mother warned me never to kiss a man. So I had a baby at sixteen and I had never kissed a man. I thought I would never get in trouble because you only had babies when you kissed people and I hadn't kissed him. You may laugh, but that is the truth!

My daughter is now the mother of four children. God has redeemed her and redeemed me. I can look at my child, a gorgeous young woman whom God gave me, and thank God for her because God still gave her to me though she was conceived in sin. God assured me there were no illegitimate children—that He was the Father of all life. I can rejoice in that grown woman today. I don't look at her as a continual reminder of my sin, but as a gift of God—that's what redemption is all about.

But as far as the world is concerned, I should be walking around for the rest of my life with my head hanging down in shame. How could I stand up and be a preacher today?

NO GROUND

Because the girl who had that baby died—back there on Calvary, in Jesus Christ. The woman standing to preach is a total new creation and I'm still discovering and learning who she really is in Christ.

I had to get a whole new attitude to bring my mind, my will, and my emotions up to the level of truth that Jesus said I was a new creature in Him. Though my baby was constantly standing before me to remind me of my sin, yet I took God's Word above what I saw, what I felt, what I tasted, touched, and smelled. I *am* a new creature; my baby is redeemed; and my whole life is entirely different.

I know that some people still remember when. Because of that, they have never got acquainted with *me*—they are too busy remembering when. I may walk into some churches and certain places, and people will say, "Man, did you know Evelyn Carter is *preaching*?"

"Aw, you're kiddin'! I remember when—"

"Yeah, but you haven't heard her now."

"No, and I don't want to. I remember when."

And look what they're missing!

God had to change my life a whole lot. I was so mean and so hateful. I despised everything and everybody and literally punched my way to adulthood. I fought everybody who looked at me funny. When I was growing up, I knew some kids who were cross-eyed. I thought they were looking at me funny. I'd say, "What are you looking at me like that for?" and I'd smack them!

I was tall. It seems like I've been five feet nine since I was eight years old! I was long and skinny and gangling and black and my mother's heartache. She and everyone else said that I'd never amount to anything—that I was the black sheep of the family. Hearing that, I went ahead and acted like it. I was programed to. I just stayed in trouble, always doing something I had no business doing.

I remember one day in school I was sent to the principal's office. That was nothing new. I was snickering and snorting and my nose was working and I was just gritting my teeth. The principal said, "You know, you're the stubbornest thing I've ever seen, and the next time I see a jackass, I'm going to apologize to it."

I went home and told my daddy that the principal called me a jackass. Of course he didn't, in so many words, but my father hated white folks so much that I knew if I told him that, he would go over there and do a job on that man. My daddy went to that school snorting and puffing just like I'd been sitting there doing. I had deliberately lied because I just wanted to see the principal get his tail beat. I was just that hung-up. I can confess it now because that mean kid died.

Many people become new creatures in Jesus and still act like they used to and think like they did before, though they really have no desire to do so. My point is that we must let the Word of God be the umpire. Don't GIVE GROUND to the enemy emotionally, mentally, or by an act of your will to be or do what you used to. Get to know who you are *now*! And stand tall.

You are not a sinner any more. Jesus paid your debt so you don't have to live in the shadow of the past and be nervous in case someone finds out about it. I don't have to overcompensate and get dressed up and try to act pretty. I can *be* beautiful in Jesus. I can be the King's kid. That sin nature, that old gal who had to fight simply because she wanted somebody to pay attention to her—she's a new creature in Christ Jesus!

Yes, I had a guilty conscience once, but the blood of Jesus Christ cleansed me from all sin. Now I can lie down at night and go to sleep peacefully. If I wake up in the morning, it's okay; if I don't, it's okay too. When bad things happen, I don't have to think, *Oh, that's God punishing me for something I did twenty-five years ago.* He's *not* that kind of God and don't let the enemy come along and fool you with that into giving him ANY GROUND.

Some people have looked at me and said, "I'd like to be like Rev. Ev and do the things for God that she does." But they don't realize where I've come from—the heartaches, the pain, the mistakes, the flubs I've made, or what it cost me to become what I am for Jesus. I'm a firm believer that the latter is going to be greater than the former.

If I'm so afraid that people won't love me if they know where I've come from, then I'm bound to that which I was. But I'm *free* from it! Jesus in me gets the glory. I don't run around and wave a flag and say, "Look at *me!*" But if the Spirit of God brings up a point in my past to share to help someone, then, if I'm not dead to it by that time, I surely do die in the process of sharing it so that God can get the glory.

15

SIGN A *UNION* CONTRACT

How does the idea of bribing God grab you? Kinda shameful? Well, haven't we sometimes heard saints implying by their prayers, "Lord, if you do this, then I'll agree to praise you?"

I can imagine God saying, "Do you mean that if I *don't* do it, you're not going to praise me?"

As for me, *I'm* going to praise God whether He does what I want or not. Why? Because He is worthy of our praise! When our wills have been possessed with God's will, we will choose to do the will of the Father and not rely on ourselves. We won't try to twist God's arm to give us something by offering Him some lip praise. We have the joy of turning constantly to Him to find out what He wants us to do. That is dependence and absolute unconditional surrender.

I dearly love this verse: "Make the Almighty your gold and the Lord your precious silver treasure" (Job 22:25). Do you know what that means? Make God the Father your source of supply. "For where your treasure is, there will your heart be also" (Matt. 6:21). We should make Jesus our secret love and God the Father our source.

If you do that, "Then you will have delight in the Almighty, and you will lift up your face to God." You will pray and God will hear you. "You shall also decide and decree a thing and it shall be established for you" (Job 22:26-28). Often we don't even know what we want; that's why we can't receive more from God.

He says, "Tell me what you want."

We say, "Oh, I just want to carry out your will."

"But what do *you* want?"

"Oh, Lord, I just want to do your will." It sounds so spiritual but it may just be a cop-out!

God voluntarily promises, "Delight yourself also in the Lord, and He will give you the desires and secret petitions of your heart" (Ps. 37:4). But if you don't know what you want, how can God give you the desires of your heart? God tells us first to decide, and then decree it—that means to say it aloud and declare it.

"Oh, I couldn't possibly do that! What if my desires are contrary to the will of God?"

You make such statements because you don't know the will of God. "For it is God Who is all the while effectually at work" (Phil. 2:13). Where? "In you—energizing and creating in you the power and desire—both to will and to work for His good pleasure and satisfaction and delight." If God is going to put His desire *in* me, then why shouldn't He ask me, "What do you desire?" He just wants us to go ahead and say it. God is only carrying out His own will if He's going to give you what you ask for, because your will and His have become one.

We have concluded that we should agree with the will of God. Then let us show ourselves to be in agreement with that will by stepping out on it and decreeing it; in that way the world will know. God promises, "I'll back you up."

The enemy of our soul GAINS GROUND when we're afraid of our own desires. We've been taught that our desires are so unholy that they could never be in conformity with the will of God.

If the Spirit of God reveals to us that our will is coinciding with the will of God, then why do we still think we must be wrong? That couldn't possibly be God because that's what *I* want! God wouldn't do that, would He? We want somebody to say, "No, you're right, He wouldn't."

Then somebody comes along and says, "Oh, yes, He would!" And we call that a person a fanatic.

We really don't understand how it is, but God *will* give us the desires of our hearts. We need to realize that our desires have been redeemed, and that we can always check out whether they are or are not of God, and whether or not they coincide with the Word of God. God said that He would confirm His Word, spoken or otherwise, in the mouth of two or three witnesses. Confirmation will come to you in time. You can always put the desire on the back burner and let it simmer. A good stew simmers a long while!

God didn't say that *you* would have to establish it. You don't have to work to make it happen. It's the Father's delight to establish His word. He said, "I am watching over My word to perform it" (Jer. 1:12). God delights in backing up His children.

Then He said, "When they make you low, you will say, There is a lifting up" (Job 22:29). I don't know if you know anything about clay while it is in process on the potter's wheel, but it is *even while the clay is being worked on* in the hands of the potter, that it rises and begins to take form and shape. People say, *"Someday,* as soon as I get to such and such an advanced spiritual state, God may use me."

Oh no. *While you are in the process of becoming,* God will use you. And whenever you feel low, God picks you up. When everybody else is putting you down, and the enemy is hacking away at you, God says, "Just trust me," and He'll cause the people to take notice of you. He'll be saying, "Have you considered my servant John or Mary or whoever?" That's what happens many times. When the enemy comes along and pounces on us, *we* want to sit down, depressed, in the mud puddles of life.

When the seed is put into the ground, it does something even in the process of dying. It shoots its roots down in order to bear its fruit later. If you dig up that seed to see whether or not it is growing, the bottom of it will have split and sent a root down. What is our root as believers? God the Father is our root.

Let's concentrate on John 15—it's really beautiful! Jesus starts out with my favorite two little words: I am. God had declared, "I AM WHO I AM and WHAT I AM, and I WILL BE WHAT I WILL BE when I get ready to be what I want to be" (Exod. 3:14, paraphrase).

"I AM the True Vine and My Father is the Vinedresser. Any branch in Me that does not bear fruit—that stops bearing—He cuts away (trims off, takes away). And He cleanses and repeatedly prunes every branch that continues to bear fruit, to make it bear more and richer and more excellent fruit" (John 15:1, 2).

Do you know anything about fruit trees or grapevines? After abundant fruit has been borne, the vinedresser comes along and snips branches back till the tree looks like it's almost dead. You would think that it would never bear another fruit. But the fruit that is borne on the tree comes from the *life* that is in the tree—the sap. It doesn't depend on the snipped-off branches.

We go through cycles in our walk with Jesus. When we finish a cycle, we naturally come to a place of rest. That is something we Christians don't know enough about—how to rest in God. The enemy of our souls, as well as human life and circumstances, has programed us to believe that if we aren't continuously *doing something*, we are going to get thrown out on the dung heap. When we have completed a cycle and God is generously giving us an opportunity to rest, (or sort of be in neutral) right away the enemy comes along and says, "God isn't talking to you. You don't feel the Spirit like you used to feel Him, do you? You must have stepped out of the will of God."

We immediately agree and GIVE GROUND to the enemy. "Oh, yes, what do you suppose I did? I don't feel all excited in Jesus at this moment. How did I get out of the will of God?" Then we start complaining to God because He doesn't seem to be saying anything to us.

Men put their horses or mules out to pasture to refresh them. They don't work them continuously; they give them a chance to recuperate. As soon as we don't have an excited feeling, or the hair isn't standing up on our arms, or we don't have goose pimples, right away we think God must have left us.

He assures us that He is our *constant* companion; He abides in us. So whether I ever feel Him, or ever get thrilling sensations or glory bumps or a twitch or an itch or anything else, *God is there!* That's the reality I have to have whether I ever have the same manifestation of the Spirit of God that I had six years ago or not.

There are things that a baby believer needs that a more mature child doesn't need. We can walk by an adult and maybe just squeeze his hand on occasion, or look at him meaningfully and say, "I care." Maybe you just nod your head, or wink an eye, or indicate some kind of communication. But a child needs to be picked up and cuddled and pampered all the time. As we grow in the Lord, the things that we needed to have to experience the reality of His abiding in us when we first started to walk with Him, we don't really need. But the enemy comes along and mocks us, "Well, you're not twitching any more. You aren't close to the Lord." If you yield to those lies, you are GIVING GROUND to the enemy.

One of the saddest things I see all over this country is that born-again, Spirit-filled people are afraid of the devil. I don't understand it. Of course he has power, but I know something else—that my heavenly Daddy has more, and that my elder Brother has defeated him! He defeated him for me, and then bound him up for me, cast him away from me, and promised me power over him.

Luke 10:19 is terrific. It begins with a little word that we need to get familiar with: "Behold." It means, "Look—you want to hear some good news?" It's like a trumpet blowing—ta-ta-da-dump-da—and everybody jumps up and asks, "What's the matter?"

It says, "Behold! I have given you authority and power . . . over all the power that the enemy[possesses] ." Now that's a bit much, don't you think? God has given us what we need to back up what we have.

To do what? "To trample." What do you do when you trample something? You stomp all over it, don't you? That verse tells us that we have authority to "trample over serpents and scorpions, and (physical and mental strength and ability) over all the power that the enemy [possesses], and nothing shall in any way harm you" (Luke 10:19). If we didn't get anything more than that, we could go shouting the victory!

If Jesus is the head, and He's abiding in us, and His Word is abiding in us, then we have authority so that *nothing*, no thing, can in any way harm us.

Some people ask whether that implies that we should never be sick. 3 John 2 is the prayer of the beloved apostle for us, "I pray that you may prosper in every way and [that your body] may keep well, even as [I know] your soul keeps well and prospers." What is God's highest and best for us? To live in health. If your soul is prospering, you should expect health!

Proverbs 17:22 is a great prescription: "A happy heart is a good medicine and a cheerful mind works healing, but a broken spirit dries the bones." Get happy, rejoice in Jesus, and health will just have to flow from you. It's not God's will that you be sick. But do you know why the enemy of your soul attacks your body? Because the body houses the spirit and the mind. If your body is attacked, you get your eyes on your body, and your mind on your body, and it is a downhill road.

God said that He dwells in the praises of His people (Ps. 22:3). How can the enemy attack a praising believer? Just start praising Jesus, start taking God at His Word. It is God's desire that we be completely whole. He thought that up, I didn't!

If we abide in Christ, and the life that is in Him abides in us, the vitality that is in the root flows up through the trunk and right into the branch—that becomes the vitality of every leaf. There is no break; it is continuous communion because the life stems from the Life-giver.

If a tree is not a fruit-bearing tree, then the *leaves* are the fruit of the tree. I'd rather be fruit than leaves, but if God has ordained you to be a leaf, then be a leaf for the Lord's sake.

Jesus said, "You are cleansed and pruned already" (John 15:3). A lot of people think they must get pruned *in order* to produce, but that is not what the Word says. "You are cleansed and pruned *already* because of the Word which I have given to you—the teachings I have discussed with you."

For years I struggled. I thought the Lord was lopping off and lopping off and lopping off. Then one day I read this and I really thought it must have been newly inserted into my Bible! It is the *Word* that prunes. It is the *Word* that cleanses. "Dwell in Me and I will dwell in you.—Live in Me and I will live in you. Just as no branch can bear fruit of itself without abiding in (vitally united to) the vine, neither can you bear fruit unless you abide in Me." You can't be Christ-like without Jesus being on your inside.

But when He *is* there, He will reproduce himself in you *without your efforts*. If we live in Him, and He lives in us, He will produce His image and likeness in us, and there will be a manifestation of His image without any effort on our part. Our part is to let the life of Christ freely flow through us.

You've never seen a fruit tree in labor pains to bear fruit! It simply and quietly stands and abides. It doesn't even get upset and nervous about the climate it's placed in. The climate is an outer thing. It gets its signals from the sap on the inside, which is the life and the vitality of the tree.

When the life of Jesus is within us, we should not spend more time dealing with the climate than we do with the sap. "He Who lives in you is greater (mightier) than he who is in the world" (1 John 4:4). The climate is the world's atmosphere. You get the right atmosphere *inside*, and know who you are, and keep rejoicing and praising the Lord, and there will be, must be, an outward manifestation of health and wholeness because you are loving and living just like Jesus.

Love, joy, peace, longsuffering, temperance, goodness, gentleness—all those fruits of Galatians chapter five—are the outward manifestations that He is abiding on the inside. You don't have to labor to produce them. You can't help it. What we need is more "can't help it" Christians!

Our relationship with Jesus is a *union contract*. Do you know that you cannot break real union, you can only break communion? The enemy of our souls has convinced us that sin will break *union*. Sin can only break *communion*.

The enemy says that when you sin or do something wrong, you're not only out of the will of God, you've lost your position in Him. What we do lose is the *consciousness* that we're in Him and He's in us. We don't have that close communion. If we start listening to the enemy, right away we attempt to strive hard to get back. But the Word tells us that if we do wrong, the proper route back is to confess it; God is faithful and just to do what He has promised and forgives us (1 John 1:9).

"Lord, I'm sorry; forgive me for my sin; blot out my transgressions again in the shed blood of Jesus." And it's done. We have immediately restored communion. We never did lose our *position* as children of our Father God. We may even accept the fact that God forgives us, and Jesus forgives us, but somehow we don't forgive ourselves. That's what breaks communion. We can't seem to *feel* God any more. *When I used to pray*, we remember, *I used to have such joy. I don't feel it now*. Then you think you have to start working up until you feel what you felt way back when. Remember, you are not back there any more. You have grown. Circumstances and situations have come and gone in your life and you are not the same person.

We are forever taking our spiritual temperatures, and feeling our pulses to see how spiritual we are, how great we are, or whether we feel like we felt at some point before. We come up to people (figuratively) and stand back to back spiritually to see if we are measuring up to them. We should take our standard only from Jesus. We should not count too much on our feelings. Feelings are the voice of the body, and they can be played upon by outward expressions and forces. Circumstances affect your feelings. You can be high one minute, and the next minute you can be low. It is not that Jesus departed from you, but that you are hung up on your feelings.

Don't get the idea that you are suddenly not walking in the Spirit just because you don't feel the same high every minute. We don't walk in and out of the Spirit the way we go in and out of doors. We walk in Him, live in Him, move in Him, breathe in Him. It is a constant thing, not to be put on and off like Sunday clothes. The spiritual life is a disposition, a conscious reality that you *are* in the Spirit, totally outside of feelings.

God may have used a certain manifestation of His Spirit to get your attention in the beginning, and then you get stuck in the mud on that and refuse to move on beyond. Get to know Jesus beyond the gifts and put your confidence in Him as a person. Sometimes God has to deliberately take a sign away from us because He wants us to trust our relationship with Him and not something we can feel, touch, taste, see or smell—purely of the senses.

Jesus said He came in to stay and make us His permanent dwelling place. You might say, "But I'm not getting anything when I read the Word." Read it anyhow. Keep on reading it. Take it in. It is food for your spirit. We keep taking our meals sometimes even when we are not hungry—and our coffee breaks, coke breaks, and snack breaks. We'd do better if we took spiritual breaks, even read three-minute snacks of Scripture. It would do more for us than any coffee break! "Take five," as they say, when the enemy is really coming at you and you're finding yourself getting terribly discouraged. That's the time to start praising the Lord and praying in the Spirit.

"There are too many people around; I can't do it," you try to excuse yourself. Go into the bathroom if you have to! Get away where you can be by yourself and talk to Jesus. "I don't know what to say to Him." Since you don't know, let the *Spirit* do the praying. He knows what to say. He knows more about what you need than you'll ever be conscious of.

Jesus said, "If a person does not dwell in Me, he is thrown out as a [broken-off] branch and withers. If you live in Me—abide vitally united to Me—and My words remain in you and continue to live in your hearts, ask whatever you will and it shall be done for you. When you bear (produce) much fruit, My Father is honored and glorified; and you show and prove yourselves to be true followers of Mine. I have loved you [just] as the Father has loved Me; abide in My love—continue in His love with Me" (John 15:6-9).

I'm so glad that Jesus never falls out of love with us—that there is *nothing* that we can do that will cause Him to do so. Even in the midst of our worst, the thing that He wants to manifest to us more than anything else is how much He loves us.

16

ENEMY GROUND TACTICS

Sometimes we have a strange reaction to God's love. In our minds we know we are forgiven and cleansed, but one of the enemy's GROUND tactics is to make us feel that we want to be punished. We resist anybody loving us. We draw away from God and push Him from us at the very time we need Him and when He is wanting to express His love to us.

Have you ever seen a kid when he's done something really wrong, and you want to pick him up and love him and say it's okay—and he doesn't want to hear it? His vibrations seem to tell us, "I'm not good enough to be loved. You don't know what I did."

"Yeah, I do," says God to us.

When you have the Jesus kind of love, and you're trying to show that kind of love, you don't ever have to try to convict anyone of their sins. Just love them! When you are giving love, and they think they don't deserve love, it is just like when the Lord is trying to love us and we know

123

we don't deserve it; still He's there, steadily dishing it out, pouring it on us. The enemy comes along and whispers, "You're not worthy of that love."

Then be bold and say, "Yeah, I know, but *Jesus is my worthiness!*" And go ahead and receive His love whether you feel like you're worthy or not. If you don't, you will GIVE GROUND to the enemy. People need to be reminded of their worthiness in Jesus. He took our filthiness unto himself and gave us a robe, wrapped us in His righteousness, and presented us to the Father as His trophies.

Belittling ourselves is another one of the enemy's GROUND tactics. There is no difference in importance among the members of the body of Christ. We are all one. There are no big "I's" and no little "you's" in the kingdom. The apple at the top of the tree is just as important as the apple on the bottom branch.

If you leave the fruit on the tree until the tree is ready to give up the fruit, it will give it up without a struggle, and it will be sweeter. But if you try to jerk the fruit off the tree before it's ripe, the tree will resist. When it's ripe, it will have a fragrance too. You can tell mature fruit by its smell. We need more ripe "smelly" Christians!

Fruit bearing is always the manifestation of an internal relationship with Jesus. People think, *I have to work to produce fruit.* No. Just get into an intimate relationship with Jesus and you can't help bearing fruit. Jesus said, "I came that they may have and enjoy life, and have it in abundance—to the full, till it overflows" (John 10:10).

If you truly live out this abiding life in Jesus, anything you have is His, and anything He has is yours. If you think that anything is privately yours, and clench it in your hot, little hand like a child—whether it is your mind, or your spirit, or your body, your relationship to someone else, or even your relationship to Jesus, and you declare, "This is mine!" it is GROUND for the enemy of your soul to try to get it away from you.

But everything you give to Jesus, He owns; therefore, there is NO GROUND for the enemy in it. You may say, "But this is *my* wife; this is *my* house; this is *my* car; this is *my* church or ministry; this is *my* . . . this is *my*. . . ." When you say such things you are inviting an enemy attack.

But when you say, "Lord, I thank you for the privilege of raising *your* child; I thank you for the privilege of living in *your* house; I thank you, Lord, for being able to lie down in the bed that *you* gave me," the enemy can't do anything with these things because *they don't belong to you*. They are the Lord's already.

Hal Hill has a fantastic chapter in his book, *How To Live Like a King's Kid*, about his only child (she was already an adult) who got sick. They had everybody across the country praying for her. Word came to Hal from Bethesda Naval Hospital to get there quickly because she was dying. Hal is a man of faith—he not only preaches and teaches but practices faith. He just sat there and began to fuss with God.

"Lord, I believe you for healing; I believe you for wholeness; I believe you for this and for that." He said, "Lord, that's my child lying there."

The Lord spoke to him, "If that's *your* child, prepare for her funeral; if she's *mine*, prepare for a miracle."

NO GROUND

Hal said, "Thank you, Jesus, for my *sister*." (She was a Christian too.) "She is *your child!*" Hal gave her up and God raised her up. She is alive today.

That's very, very real. Anything that *you* lay hold to becomes GROUND for the enemy. If you're holding on to your life and trying to protect yourself, when you should be totally given to God, that's GROUND for the enemy to walk on and trample you. If you know that your life is hid with Christ in God, and you've given yourself—body, mind, soul, spirit, emotions, passions, desires, actions, reactions, your social life, your sex life, your financial life, your academic life—all to the Lord, what can the enemy use? What can he do? Nothing! Again, it is really so simple.

How about when other people pick your pocket or rob your house? If all you have is already given to Him, whatever happens, happens to *Jesus' possessions*, not yours. I travel a lot. When I leave, I lock the door and say, "Lord, I commit the place into your hands. Everything in there you've given me. If you don't keep it, it won't be kept. If you choose to let somebody else have it, it's all right because I know you must have something better for me." And I leave.

I come back, open the door, walk in, and say, "Thank you, Jesus. You kept everything intact. Evidently you don't want me to have any better, so I'm going to enjoy this." This is very freeing. Sometimes I'm gone five and six weeks at a time, and I don't worry about what's going on back home.

I even commit my house plants to the Lord. I don't arrange to have anybody water my plants, so I've always

told my plants how much Jesus loves them, and how much
I love them. When I get ready to leave them, I give them a
last drink of water. I say, "I'm going to be away for a long
time; you're not going to get any more water, so drink
slowly. Remember that Jesus is going to take care of you
until I get back." I have never come home to a dead plant.
There's often a new leaf on one of my plants to greet me
when I return.

I have one plant, I don't know what the fancy name for
it is, but when I got it, it was small. Now it is over eight
feet tall. I had to cut it down and re-root it. Now I'm going
to have four plants out of that one. When I cut it down I
said, "I'm not hurting you; I love you; you're special to me.
But I have to do this in order for you to become better and
for there to be more of you." (Just like Jesus said He
prunes us so that we might bring forth more fruit.)

And when I take a plant out of a crowded pot, I tell it,
"I'm not angry with you. I'm not taking you away from
your mother to be malicious, but I have enough confidence
that you have grown to the place where you can stand on
your own." Then I put it in a pot all by itself in order for it
to become what it is supposed to be. A lot of good spiritual
illustrations from that!

The way to take the GROUND right out from under the
enemy is to saturate yourself with the Scriptures. Read
the Bible regularly and obediently in order to know the
will of God. That's why we're told to let God's Word dwell
in us richly. We need to "eat" the Word of God so that we
can find out His directions for *every* area of our
lives—marriage, sex, finances, social life, academic life,
spiritual life—because He said He has given us everything

we need for life and godliness through the knowledge of Jesus Christ.

If we learn to abide in Him, and turn every day and every moment of our lives over to Him, the enemy will have NO GROUND in us. Jesus Christ can and will be Lord as we *let* Him be Lord over every situation. If He's the head, then recognize Him as the head; the body never tells the head what to do. It's the head that works through the body. Praise God!

17

PROGRAMING WITH THE WORD

Today, David the psalmist might have put Psalm 119:11 this way: "I have programed the computer of my heart with your Word, O God. Therefore it will read out 'No sin against God.' "

When a computer gets reprogramed, something new has to replace what was there previously. One of the chief ways of not GIVING GROUND to the enemy, is to ingest God's Word—to chew it, swallow it, let it become a part of us, and live in the reality of it. We must begin to act like we believe it. We need the infilling of the Holy Spirit to reveal Jesus Christ in depth because it is the *Spirit* who opens up the *Word* to us.

Anyone who reads the Word at all gets something out of it, even if he reads it only from an intellectual viewpoint. If you read it as a recently born-again believer, you'll get more out of it. But when you receive the infilling of the Holy Spirit, and you read the Word because the Holy Spirit is the author of the Word, all of the Bible takes on an even more tremendous meaning. If you take one passage of Scripture and read it every day for seven days, I guarantee that you'll get new hidden truth out of it every day.

The Word transforms; the Word renews; the Word brings reality to you. But you have to take action on that Word and apply it. You'll never know just by reading in the Word of God that signs and wonders shall follow them that believe (Mark 16:17) until you step out on that Word. Then the signs *do* follow you. It won't be just mental assent but actuality.

When I came into the PTL TV studio to do a taping one morning, one of the hostesses met me. I said, "Hi, how are you doing?"

She replied, "Oh, I'm feeling lousy today."

"What's the matter?"

"I have a bad sinus headache."

I said, "Let's do something about it." She looked at me strangely. I said, "Do you mind sitting down for a hot minute and taking off your hat?"

She said, "No, God knows I'd do anything right now for help." We sat her down and she said she also had a back problem. She had slipped in the driveway and wrenched her back.

I said, "Well, let's take care of the head first." And the Lord marvelously opened up her sinuses right away. One of her legs was about an inch and a half shorter than the other. Without even praying, just calling on the name of Jesus, we saw that leg shoot right out and become even with the other. God took all of her pain away. And I hadn't even got to the studio yet!

That gal had had a headache for two weeks. How sad! There's nothing worse than a sinus headache because it has the same kind of effect as a migraine headache—you feel almost blind with pain and your temples are throbbing so hard that you can't think. I said to our co-workers, "To be in a place where there is so much of God's power, and to walk around sick, without taking time for healing, is inconsistent." *We're so busy working and doing our job for Jesus that we can't take time to be ministered to by Jesus himself!* It happens all the time in the body of Christ. We get caught up doing what we think we ought to do for God and don't take time out to enter in with Him and have our personal needs met.

What good does it do for me to teach others about the realities of God if I don't apply them to myself? Paul said that he took heed to himself, that after proclaiming the gospel to others, he himself might not become a castaway (1 Cor. 9:27). There are many members of the body of Christ who can easily tell somebody else what they ought to do, but they won't go to God for their own needs. Why? Because the church has given us the impression that *we're* not important, that it is selfish to pray for ourselves. That gives the enemy GROUND.

You can't give somebody something you don't have. There is a little saying in Christian circles, even in Spirit-filled circles, that real *JOY* is Jesus first, Others second, and Yourself last. That's a nice motto but that is not reality nor is it truly biblical. Surely it is *Jesus first*, but then it's Ourself, and then it's You. That also spells joy and is closer to reality. The Bible says we should love our neighbor *as ourselves*, which implies that self-love, in the purest sense, normally comes first and is a standard by which we love others. You can't give somebody something you don't have. If you don't go and get your own tank filled, or enter in and have that time with Jesus, how can you share Him with somebody else? An old mind-set that you have been taught all your life is that you are the last person who should be considered.

Jesus said you're the *first* person you should consider: "Come unto me. . . ." He is asking for a first person response.

Well, come for what?

For *your* needs. Then you can be open and sensitive to minister to somebody else's needs. But if you have a blinding headache, or an ache or pain that you haven't come to Jesus for, your testimony is less than when you can tell someone, "I know the Lord heals because He healed me!"

Sure, the healing that you had twenty-five years ago is fantastic. But the greatest testimony is what Jesus has done for you *today*.

That's why we are told to let the Word of God have its home in our hearts and minds to dwell in us richly (Col. 3:16). Get to know the Word; walk with the Word; live in the Word; talk the Word; lie down with the Word; get up with the Word; handle the Word. "Taste and see that the Lord is good" (Ps. 34:8).

You can then become the living, walking Word. Isn't that exciting? We have the privilege of taking the Word and making it a part of us. Some people may say they don't understand it. Neither does the computer programmer understand all the technical aspects of how all that sophisticated hardware works, but he puts the program in anyway and *it works*. Put the Word of God into yourself and God will give the understanding. He can pull it out of you for a read out when the occasion arises. But if you don't feed it in, it can't come out.

Someone said there are three thousand and three hundred promises in the Bible. Somebody else said there were seven thousand and seven hundred. I don't care exactly how many there are, because the Scripture says that if everything Jesus did and said had been written (and it wasn't), the world could not contain the books (John 21:25).

I got real simple one day. I put the Bible down on the floor, took off my shoes, and stepped in the middle of the Bible. I said, "Dear Jesus, I claim every promise in this Book from cover to cover, and any others that you uttered but no one wrote down. I claim those too. I trust that the Holy Spirit will bring to my remembrance any of them whenever you know I need them. Thank you, Jesus." And I got off the Bible and picked it up. I believe God to do exactly that.

I have been in places where I needed something special from the Word of God and it has come right back to me so vividly and strongly. Though I've read the Bible many times from cover to cover, I surely don't profess to know it all. But within me I have the One who wrote it and He knows it all; therefore, He can bring anything to my remembrance (John 14:26).

Remember three things that make up the totality of personality—the mind, the will, and the emotions. In Ephesians 4:13 Paul talks about growing into maturity "which is nothing less than the standard height of Christ's own perfection—the measure of the stature of the fullness of the Christ, and the completeness found in Him." In the Scriptures it talks much about our whole heart, which is the personality of man.

David said, "With my whole heart have I sought You" (Ps. 119:10). His whole heart was his personality which included his mind, his will, and his emotions. These are the only parts that are going to live eternally. Your body is going to be put aside. Everything you got from your natural parents, you are going to leave here. Everything you get from God, you're going to take with you.

Our personality is going to live for eons and eons of ages—for eternity. We need to deal with God in our totality. In order for our minds, wills, and emotions to become one, we have to offer the whole of ourselves to the Lord so that all the barriers can be broken down and we can seek God with all of our hearts.

Here is a helpful hint: If you read the Word silently, you're only feeding your mind. If you read the Word aloud, it also gets into your heart and your emotions because you are hearing yourself. Hearing is emotional. You can reprogram yourself. All through the Gospels Jesus says, "He who has ears to hear, let him be listening" (Matt. 11:15).

When I meditate, I sit down and read. I start by reading the Word aloud. Then I sing the Word. After that I have my prayer time and then I sit in the quiet. I don't talk. I don't pray in tongues. I don't do anything. I just meditate.

Sometimes when I'm teaching a seminar, I give out the

Word and then I ask the people to take time and meditate on it. By just listening, people take part of it into their minds but it doesn't get in deep enough; I really want to minister to their spirits. For at least five minutes I want the people to sit in silence and allow what I have said to them to get down from their minds and soak into their hearts. I want it to settle in. Then I know it is committed and the Lord can work with it.

18

ONE-TRACK MIND TO JESUS

When people talk about someone having a one-track mind, it is not always a compliment. But when God applies that quality to us, defined from the Word of God as "singleness of heart and mind," it is an attitude which pleases Him—one which we should seek after.

David was a man who had singleness of heart as he sought the Lord. Likewise we should pray, "Lord, I choose to know you in your fullness; and I choose that every area of my life will respond to you. Remove any barriers that might exist between my intellect, my emotions, and my will so that when I say yes to you, I will have a *single mind*." It has to be all of me, or none of me, when I deal with the Lord.

Let's explore some of the riches of Psalm 119. David has been generous with the precious jewels. He starts out with a road map for our conduct and our conversation: "Blessed, happy, fortunate [to be envied] are the undefiled—the upright, truly sincere and blameless—in the way [of the revealed will of God]; who walk—that is, order their conduct and conversation—in [the whole of God's revealed will] the law of the Lord." Did you understand that? "Their conduct and conversation" means their actions and their oral life.

Verse 2, "Blessed are they who keep His testimonies, and who seek, inquire for and of Him and crave Him with the whole heart." That's the mind, and will, and emotions again.

"Yes, they do no unrighteousness—no willful wandering from His precepts; they walk in His ways" (v. 3).

Then David yearns, "O that my ways were directed and established to observe Your statutes—hearing, receiving, loving and obeying them! (v. 5). First of all, in order to know God's will, you have to hear it. Then you must receive it, which is simply accepting it. We may read the Scriptures but not accept what the Word of God says. I have to love it. The result is that the love will motivate me to obey the Word of God.

Verse 6 tells the results: "Then shall I not be put to shame [by failing to inherit Your promises], when I have respect to all Your commandments." Many of us have failed to inherit the promises of God simply because we don't know *what* they are. We've never bothered to take the time to find out what our inheritance in Jesus Christ is. The Word of God reveals it.

"I will praise and give thanks to You with uprightness of heart, when I shall have learned [by sanctified experiences] Your righteous judgments" (v. 7). The way to praise God is with uprightness of heart, which means singleness of mind. Do you know what sanctified experiences are? Those experiences chosen by God for you to experience so you can find out the reality of the Word. The Lord teaches by precepts and example. I go into the Scriptures and find something which will be quickened to me. I believe it, and I accept it with my whole heart. The next thing I know, I'm being tested on living out what I have just grabbed hold of.

Once the Lord said to me, "Evelyn, what hinders my people from entering into my promises?"

I was proud because I thought sure I knew the answer. "Unbelief and sin and all those things."

He said, "Nothing. There's absolutely nothing that can hinder them."

When God told the Israelites to go in and possess the land, He said, "I'll go before you and subdue your enemies." By the time they got to Jericho, everyone forty years and older who had come out of Egypt had died in the wilderness, except for Joshua and Caleb. It was the younger generation which had been born in the wilderness that entered in because the rest had failed to obey God. When they got into the city, the people there were huddled in groups with fear, because for forty years they had heard of the acts of the God of this nation. The news had gone ahead about the mighty God of the Israelites and the enemies were ready to surrender the keys to the city. But the Israelites had dragged their feet all this time about going in to inherit the land when *nothing* really hindered them.

It's the privilege of God to subdue your enemies. That gives you the right to go in and simply take the promises that God has given you. Jesus Christ has already gone before and secured everything for you.

The Word is a cleansing agent. I think that's fantastic! "Wherewith shall a young man cleanse his way? By taking heed and keeping watch [on himself] according to Your word[conforming his life to it]" (Ps. 119:9). The Scripture says that we are cleansed bý the washing of water with the Word (Eph. 5:26). Jesus said, "Sanctify them by the Truth. Your Word is Truth" (John 17:17). We are set apart for the use of God by the Word. The Word was with God in the beginning and is provided for our cleansing.

David said, "With my whole heart have I sought You, inquiring for and of You, and yearning for You; O let me not wander or step aside[either in ignorance or willfully] from Your commandments" (Ps. 119:10). Have you ever asked the Lord just to keep you because you want to be kept?

"Lord, I choose to be kept regardless of what happens. I want to be kept safe against my own desires. I want to be kept even against my own will—even if something should come up, and I might at that moment decide that I don't want to do it, Lord, I want to *insure* that I want to be kept. I make my choice as of this day. I choose to be kept by you, Lord, in every situation; and Lord, I'm holding you responsible for keeping me because no way can I keep myself." There are so many things that come along to tempt us away from God; but if you've asked the Lord to keep you, you can rest assured that He is going to do just that.

If we don't clearly know the voice of God and have a close relationship with Him, many are going to be led astray. The Word says that in the last days many will talk like Jesus, and there are going to be lying wonders and signs, pretending and delusive, and people are going to be chasing after them (2 Thess. 2:9). There are thousands of voices in the land, but there is only one Holy Spirit.

So many members of the body of Christ are getting suckered into other things even while trying to be more spiritual. You can never get any more spiritual than Jesus Christ, because it pleased God the Father that in Jesus all the divine attributes and all spirituality should dwell and remain permanently (Col. 1:19).

Sheep never just stray; they eat themselves away. A sheep doesn't look up and start figuring, "Oh, I'm going to yonder mountain and get lost." It just starts nibbling and nibbling. It lifts up its head only high enough to see where the next bunch of grass is. It just keeps eating and eating and eating and eats itself astray.

Don't run after every sign. Don't run after every ministry. Develop a solid relationship with Jesus. Realize that you cannot conduct your own life. You have given it to Jesus. Before you take a trip, go to a church, go to a teaching, or anything else, ask Jesus: "Lord, is that where *you* want me? Is this what you choose?" I don't care if someone else says, "Oh, she or he is so anointed." They might be telling the truth. But where *you* want to be is in the will of God. You won't know where the will of God is for you unless you ask Him.

I believe I have a good mind. I'm not bragging on myself but on Jesus when I say that. But I ask Him every morning, "Lord, what would you have me wear today?" I don't even go to the store and buy clothes unless I ask

Jesus, "What do you want me to buy? Don't let me buy anything stupid or spend money that you don't want me to spend." If I don't have any leading to buy, I don't buy. Every nickel that God gives me, I give back to Him because it belongs to Him. I ask, "Now Lord, tell me what to do with it and how to spend it." If He doesn't tell me, I don't spend it. If He does, I don't argue with Him.

On the occasion when I was given the automobile, that morning I got up and as usual asked the Lord, "What do you want me to wear today?"

He said, "Put on a red skirt, white blouse, and a black jacket."

I said, "Are you serious?" Because when I pack my bag, I always say, "Lord, you pick out what I should put in that suitcase." And when I had packed it, the combination that I had in mind for that red skirt was not a white blouse. But I felt the Lord insisting.

When the Lord unexpectedly gave me the car, someone remarked that the car was just the color of my skirt—the bottom of the car was red. The roof of the car was white like my blouse, and I had on a black velvet jacket—I was told, *"You'll* put the *black* in it!" So I was in perfect matching colors: red, white, and black.

I'm simply making the point that you should spend time with God. Put Him into your practical everyday life. As David said, we should conduct our lives by bringing them into conformity with God's Word. Of course I couldn't go to the Scripture and find out if I should wear a red skirt, white blouse, and black jacket. But when God planned the vestments for the priests, *they* went before the Lord and He gave them the specifics down to the very colors, the fabrics, the jewels (accessories!), and He anointed with the Spirit the workers who made them so they would do what they were doing in power as unto Him.

"Oh, that's so silly," you may be saying. "I have a mind of my own. I ought to know what kind of clothes I should put on."

Let Jesus answer you, not me: "Without Me you can do absolutely nothing" (John 15:5).

I'm God's child. I'm God's ambassador; I want to look good for God, my Father. If you take your sons and daughters into the department store and pick out the clothes that you think they look best in, why can't my heavenly Daddy do as much for me—and for you? Get to know God intimately. As you get your heart, mind, and emotions filled with the Word of God, there won't be any room for the enemy to infiltrate your life with his negative thoughts because you will be constantly consumed with God and in the process of renewing your mind. Never get your eyes off Him.

The only way our spiritual inward man can grow is by getting the proper nourishment from the Word of God. Most of us have neglected our spirits and so have great big bodies and puny spirits. Whenever we get into trouble, we have a puny spirit to do a great big job. The Word of God feeds the spirit into health and strength.

David cries out, "Show me Your ways, O Lord; teach me Your paths" (Ps. 25:4). And the Lord answers, "I, the Lord, will instruct you and teach you in the way you should go; I will counsel you with My eye upon you" (Ps. 32:8). That is a promise you can lay hold of. The Lord is ever so willing to counsel with us, but we have to give Him the opportunity to communicate with us.

We must be careful about one thing. God deals with individuals. The way God has for *me* to walk might not be the way God has for *you* to walk. What God might require from me, He might not require from you because we are not doing identical things; but the basic truths and requirements are the same. Search for Him with your whole heart. Don't be fragmented in any area of your life in your relationship with Jesus.

David *chose* to meditate on God's precepts, and *chose* to delight himself in God's statutes. His determination was "I will not forget Your Word," (Ps. 119:16) and "I will observe Your Word." There was nothing namby-pamby about David's dealings with the Lord.

With such a foundational relationship with the Lord, David could surely pray, "Open my eyes . . ." (Ps. 119:18). When you read the Word and pray, you can ask the Lord to quicken your spirit to perceive the truths so that the whole of you will accept the Word of God and respond. And respond immediately, while it's fresh—out of choice, out of your will, and emotionally.

Many times when the Word of God is going forth, it pricks you in the heart, right in the core of your being. At such times the most logical reaction is panic. The enemy of our souls is so slick that he GAINS GROUND by making you think everybody can see your inward being and know that you are naked and bleeding. That's only your pride and self-centeredness to think that everybody is paying attention to you. But that's a signal that you need to do business with God alone and respond immediately to His Word. Never mind the opinions of others.

We need to learn to love single-mindedly, as God loves us. When we choose to love as He loves, there are no pre-set standards of mind or heart or emotions for anybody to have to measure up to before we can love them. Too often we love people only from our little arenas, or our social circles, because they "fit" our comfortable standards. But the Christ whom we serve doesn't put up such fences. That frees everybody. That frees you to love the alcoholic, the prostitute, your own stubborn husband, your impossible wife, your wayward children, right where they are.

Many fathers alienate their sons because maybe dad wears his hair in a crew cut and son wears his hair to the shoulders. Dad can't accept his son because he doesn't conform to his standards. The bone of contention becomes *hair*—ridiculous! They allow the enemy to HAVE GROUND and sow seeds of discord to alienate two people whom God has chosen to be together.

As a young woman needing friends, and because of my background, I had a tendency to pull people to me. I had filled my life with people and things. "Evelyn," the Lord said, "I want you to give me all your relationships; I want to be Lord of your social life." I had given Him everything but my social life. He said, "*I* want to choose your friends."

I said, "Okay, Lord, I just commit them all to you."

He said, "Your life is full of haphazardness. I want to take all the haphazardness out and bring a permanence into your life from now on."

It was kind of scary at first. He took away only those

things and those people who had really caused me problems. "There is a friend who sticks closer than a brother" (Prov. 18:24). You won't know that means God if you have everybody else occupying His space. You have to be willing to let go. That's why we have to let Him open our eyes to new areas He wants to deal with in us.

God said we should learn to delight ourselves in Him. Often we delight ourselves in everything else but Him. "Delight" means "to have fun." Do you know you can have fun with Jesus? I have never had so much fun in my life as I do just sharing Jesus with people and watching them respond to Him. Having fun is the ability to have a good time without any repercussions or having to pay the consequences for having it. When you're enjoying Jesus, you can have a genuinely good time.

Do you feel weak? The Word of God is the place to go. "Strengthen me according to Your Word" (Ps. 119:28).

"I will [not merely walk, but] run the way of Your commandments, when You give me a heart that is willing" (Ps. 119:32). How many times have you prayed, "I really don't want to do this, but Lord, make me willing to be willing"? When we ask Him, God will even give us that willingness, and then we'll *run with joy* in His way.

David's next prayer was for understanding, so that he could observe God's Word with his whole heart—his total personality. When you hide the Word in your heart, you can approach God in a brand new way. You can be bold, even daring. You can ask God to prove His Word to you. "Establish Your word and confirm Your promise to Your servant" (Ps. 119:38). Then watch Him do it!

Job had a real controversy with God. What he knew

about God and what he saw being manifested seemed like two different things. You can say boldly to God, "Lord, I don't see your Word being made manifest. Prove your Word to me." He's only waiting for the opportunity to back up His Word. But if you don't ever get around to asking Him, how will you ever know it to be true?

We see David reaching higher and higher levels of maturity in His prayers before God in Psalm 119. "Teach me good judgment, wise and right discernment and knowledge, for I have believed [trusted, relied on and clung to] Your commandments" (Ps. 119:66). One of the things that we need more than anything else these days is the gift of discernment. We need to know what is of God, and what is not.

Right now America is guilty of two great abominations (among many) before God: homosexuality and witchcraft. Not only in society at large, but even in some of the churches, people are embracing homosexuality. One of the objectives of the ERA (Equal Rights Amendment) is that homosexuals will not only be able to marry, but to adopt children. We need discernment! We can ask for it and expect to receive it from God.

Paul prayed that the eyes of our hearts may be flooded with light (Eph. 1:18). That is our right. James said, "You do not have because you do not ask" (James 4:2). If you get into God's Word, you can find out what you can ask God for. He said He didn't want us to be ignorant of the devices of the enemy. Even if I don't understand something when I read it, I pray like this: "Lord, I've accepted this, but I don't understand it. Show me what you are talking about. Make this plain to me." Don't be ashamed to admit it.

The "mind gifts" are becoming more prevalent in the body of Christ today because discerning of spirits, the word of wisdom, and the word of knowledge work through the faculty of the mind. Whoever has control of the mind has lordship over the body. Whoever controls the tongue controls the mind. That is why all these things have to be brought under the lordship of the Godhead.

The key to singleness of mind, as David said, is "Let me be so in tune with Your Word that I will bring my life into conformity with Your Word." That will include both our desires and our actions. God cares about every part of our lives. Choose to make Him Lord of all and He will make you single-minded for His glory.

19

LISTEN TO DADDY

One day as I entered a building for a speaking ministry, someone thoughtfully handed me a gorgeous camellia in full bloom with another little bud beside it on the stem. I looked at it with wonder and praise to the Creator. I counted the petals—there were over twenty, in three layers like a rose. And all the beauty of the mature flower was locked up in a tight little bud at the beginning.

I thought of the wonder of a new-born baby. When a man-child is born, he can weigh as little as three pounds. You could hold him in the palm of your hand. But everything necessary for that man-child to become a six-foot-four adult of two hundred and forty pounds exists already as potential within him. The only thing remaining is to let him be nurtured and developed. He will never get anything new. He will just develop what he has from birth.

Everything we will ever need has been locked up in us through Jesus Christ. All we have to do is live and abide in

Him, use what we have, and develop. We do not have to look for anything new.

Peter tells us that in having received Jesus Christ into our lives, we have all we need resident within us. "For His divine power has bestowed upon us all things that [are requisite and suited] to life and godliness, through the (full, personal) knowledge of Him Who called us by and to His own glory and excellence (virtue)" (2 Pet. 1:3). It is up to us to study the Word and find out what wonderful things we possess, to act like we have them and to use them. The world will know Jesus because we will develop into His "flower-image." It's not a struggle; it's a being and an unfolding in a natural, yet supernatural, way.

I'm trying to arm you and outfit you in some strategic areas so that you don't have to give the enemy ANY GROUND. The reason why we do GIVE GROUND is because we simply don't know who we are, or what we possess, and because there are so many unsettled things in us.

The song: "Whatever it takes, I'm willing," is my testimony. I think I've known ever since I was a little girl of three that I was supposed to do something for God, that I wasn't ordinary. I somehow always knew that God was my Daddy. I told my own father, even at that age, that he was not my father; he was just the instrument God used to bring me into this world. I totally rejected my natural father because I was mad at him for taking me away from God to be born in this world. I don't know where I got that idea, but that was the reason I never liked him. My whole idea, all my life, was to get back to God, wherever He was, and whatever it cost me. I somehow knew that I was a stranger in this place—the world. It took Jesus to tell me how to get back to my Father God, why I was here, and what I was supposed to do while I was here.

When I really met the Lord, I already knew an awful lot about Jesus because I grew up in the context of the church. But I never paid Jesus much attention because I was concentrating on God as my Daddy. Then I found I couldn't get back to the Father without Jesus. There is no other way to God.

Jesus said that if you come any other way, you're a thief and a robber (John 10:1). If you want to get into the presence of God, Jesus is the door. It is not by meditation or psychic powers—only through the blood of Jesus can you be born of the Spirit and be brought into right relationship with God the Father. We must have that settled.

Philip said to the Lord one day, "Show us the Father—cause us to see the Father" (John 14:8).

And Jesus said, "Have I been with all of you so long a time and do you not recognize and know Me yet, Philip? Any one who has seen Me has seen the Father" (John 14:9). Why? "Because I am in the Father and the Father is in Me." It takes Jesus to introduce you to His Daddy.

When Jesus ushered me into the presence of God, I knew I was home; I was back where I belonged.

I had fought going into the ministry for years and years because of my denominational background. You may know how Baptists feel about lady preachers. But God put an unmistakable call on my life. I was a good Baptist, and I was even more loyal to my Baptist doctrines than I was to Jesus. I squirmed, and hollered, and kicked against my call to preach and settled for becoming a good missionary—which the church accepted. I became a Sunday school teacher too. I became president of the usher board. I did all the things that the church would accept, but it wasn't acceptable to God. I really tried with my man-approved detours but I just didn't have any peace in my heart.

One day I said to the Lord, "God, if I can't be free enough to do the thing that you want me to do, I really don't have any purpose for living." And that's exactly where He wanted me. I had finally got to the place of absolute surrender. I had been so miserable. I loved Jesus; I was filled with the Spirit of God; I was doing all the good things. To keep from getting into the healing ministry, I went into nursing. I thought I was going to end up being a medical missionary.

Oh, I was good! I was so dedicated as a scrub nurse. I'd get in there and ask Jesus which of my instruments I needed and what was going to happen during the case so I could have all the extras I would need. Instead of letting the orderlies go and get my patients, I'd get them myself. If they had to get them because I didn't have enough time, I'd set up my tables in a hurry and go out and talk with them, and pray with them, and tell them that Jesus loved them, and that we were going to be praying during their operation.

But I was still out of the *perfect* will of God because He had called me to preach and to teach. You can be miserable even doing good things if they are not God's highest and best. I finally died to the opinions of my family, members of my church and others. I said, "God, it's you and me all the way."

Then the Lord said, "You tell them what I have in store for you."

I went to my pastor, who loved me, and who had trained me from a little girl. He was a much older man, a good Bible teacher, and called me "daughter" all the time. "I have something to tell you," I said. "And you're not going to be very happy about it!"

He inquired, "What is it, daughter?"

I had been a rather controversial figure in my church, to say the least. I got saved in the Baptist church, sitting in the fourth pew on the right hand side. I got filled with the Holy Spirit in the Baptist church on the fourth pew. I spoke in tongues on the fourth pew, sitting in the Baptist church. I started laying hands on the sick in the Baptist church on the fourth pew. The church establishment was totally upset with me. At that time I was in a key position in the church—I was the director of youth.

God stepped up the controversy when the whole youth department of a hundred and twenty young people were baptized in the Holy Spirit, speaking in tongues, surrounding the fourth pew in the Baptist church. The church people just knew there wasn't any such thing! But when it happened, people said they saw flames of fire leaping from the top of the building. Someone turned in the alarm and two fire departments came with all their equipment. The Holy Spirit was just laying folk down and picking them up and carrying them across the room.

Obviously, I was like a bad little girl in the Baptist church. You know how bad kids are treated? Every time they do something they end up in the principal's office.

Well, I was bad in church. Every time I turned around, the pastor was calling me, "Daughter, may I see you in my office?"

On one such occasion he said, "You know, daughter, I'm a little concerned."

I responded, "How's that?"

He said, "Because the Lord is coming in the back door."

"The back door?"

"Yes."

I answered, "Pastor, you asked me to pray for the Holy Spirit to move in our church. You didn't tell me which door you wanted Him to come in."

He said, "Everything is happening to the young people, and there's nothing happening to the older ones."

I said, "That's because they're so hardened and they don't believe. The youngsters believe the Word of God when they are taught." (I knew he was referring to the hundred and twenty kids from the balcony whom God had brought down to the third and fourth pews and filled with the Holy Spirit while the pastor was standing on the platform telling them there was no such thing.)

He continued, "Daughter, that stuff you've got on the board, I know a lot of theologians who would call you to task about that. Where did you get your theology?"

"My *what?*" I thought that was some kind of disease. I didn't know anything about theology. I was just doing what was in the Word of God.

Anyway, I went ahead to tell him, "The Lord is calling me into the ministry to be an evangelist and a teacher."

He just sat there stunned. Finally he recovered his wits and asked, "Well, how about telling the church on

Wednesday night?"

But Wednesday night there were only a few people in prayer meeting, and God said, "No, I don't want to do this thing in a corner. You tell them on Sunday morning when the church is full."

We had 1600 people in our church, and I sure didn't want to get up in front of all of them and make any confession. That Sunday morning I sat there with my heart pounding and the Holy Spirit started working on me. I sat and I sat and I sat. I wiggled and I sweated and I shook and the whole bit. Finally I tiptoed to the front, called my pastor to the side, and whispered, "Now!"

He said, "Okay" but went on and on with the service. The enemy tried to tell me that he wasn't going to let me talk at all. But just before the pastor got ready for the benediction, he finally said, "I'd like you all to take your seats. There is a young woman of our church who has a statement to make."

There was my momma and everybody sitting there. And my closest girl friend whom I had sat beside for ten years. We had gone to school as children and been in the same classes. Then we became members of the same church and sat on the fourth pew on the right hand side.

I got up in fear and trembling and prayed all the way across the front of the church. I got to the mike and gulped out my statement. From that moment on, I ceased to be the "fair-haired girl" in my church and even my dear friend who had sat beside me for ten years stood up and waved good-bye to me, walked out, and never spoke another word to me for three solid years—simply because I had to obey God.

It requires a cost to take God seriously. But my theme became, "Whatever it takes, I'm willing." God *will* speak to you through His Word. But people may not be happy with you when you begin to take the Scriptures and live them. Oh, just to study them is fine and harmless. But don't talk too much about your personal relationship with Jesus, they advise. If you believe the Scriptures and start acting like you believe God, it is liable to cost you something—it is liable to cost you everything!

That's why Jesus said to count the cost. No man begins to build a building unless he first sits down to figure the price (Luke 14:28-30). If you want to be popular with people, and you want everyone to like you, stay away from Jesus. Because many people will not like you. They didn't like our Christ so how do you expect them to love you, if you've fallen in love with Him? If you think it's going to be a bed of roses, and you'll never have another moment of trouble, I would advise you to give it up now because that is not reality.

Don't think that because you seek the infilling of the Holy Spirit, and receive Him, that all your cares and woes will surely be over. That's not the truth. You'll have heartaches and tears, but the difference is that there will be somebody with you in the midst of it (Isa. 43:2), and that's Jesus and His enabling power. Don't be surprised if the enemy of your soul is going to try to do everything to get you back into his clutches and GAIN BACK GROUND that he lost. He only attacks believers because he doesn't have to attack the ones who already belong to him.

The enemy will attack you with discouragement. Paul

said, "I know how to be abased and live humbly in straitened circumstances, and I know also how to enjoy plenty and live in abundance. I have learned in any and all circumstances, the secret of facing every situation, whether well-fed or going hungry, having a sufficiency and to spare or going without and being in want" (Phil. 4:12). He said he knew what it meant to be perplexed, in situations where it seems like there is no way out; he was beaten and threatened, in prison and all kinds of troubles (2 Cor. 11:23-27), but he rejoiced in it all because it was "for the gospel's sake."

One of the first things you have to learn if you want to go on with Jesus is how to die to self, your personal ambitions, your own desires apart from Him. Sometimes the perfect will of God will lead you through the valley, but He is your enabler, and your equipment, and your equipper. Anything that He chooses you for, you can do through Christ.

Jesus cried to the Father, "I don't want to go to the cross. Father, if there's any other plan, tune me in on it. Nevertheless. . ." (Luke 22:42, paraphrase). We, too, have to come to the place of our "neverthelesses" because Jesus said, "Nevertheless, not My will, but Thy will be done. If there's no other way, then I'm willing to go all the way."

He went to the cross; He went to the grave; He went through hell; He went through death; He arose the victor!

And because of what He did, each one of us who believe on Him is born crucified. You are born crucified at the same time you are born again. But everything in us does not know that it is crucified, so we have to notify our minds, and intellects, and wills, and emotions that we're already crucified. I'm dead to the old way of looking at things. I'm dead to the old way of reacting to things. I'm dead to my desires, to my ambitions. But I'm alive unto the Lord Jesus Christ!

Listen to your heavenly Daddy and don't settle for anything less than God's highest and God's best, no matter what standards the world may falsely set up. Build on God's GROUND and don't let the enemy even rent a space!

20

IN THE
PRESENCE OF GOD

I found out from my personal experience that the place where I am the most happy, where I have the most joy, is *in the presence of God*.

Don't let the enemy of your soul convince you that you can't live in God's presence all the time. You *can* live in the presence of God moment by moment. You can live in it; you can play in it; you can relax in it; you can stand and work in the presence of God. The presence of God is really resident *within* you because that's where the secret place of the Most High is. His dwelling place is where you find reality—the presence of God.

How practical His presence really is! You can drive your car in it; you can go shopping in it; you can buy food in the presence of God; you can pick out the things that you want for your life—cars and everything—in the presence of God; you can eat your meals in the presence of God; you can lie down at night in the presence of God; you can dream dreams in the presence of God; you can wake up in the morning in the presence of God. You don't *ever* have to get out of the presence of God. Why? *Because He is in you!* (Ps. 139:7-12).

You might not always be conscious of the presence of God, but you have to know beyond a shadow of a doubt that you do abide in it. "He who dwells in the secret place. . ." (Ps. 91). What is the secret place? In the Spirit. We are to live in the Spirit and move in the Spirit. Paul said, "In Him we live and move and have our being" (Acts 17:28).

When you get exhausted and tired, don't try to relax on your own. Take your refreshment by getting into the presence of God. "That times of refreshing—of recovering from the effects of heat, of reviving with fresh air—may come from the presence of the Lord" (Acts 3:19). You haven't experienced real refreshment until you let the Lord refresh you. You don't know what it is to be rested and comforted until you let the Holy Spirit comfort you.

There are seven titles for the Holy Spirit in the Amplified version of John 14:26. I just love them. They are so yummy! Besides Holy Spirit, they are: Comforter, Counselor, Helper, Intercessor, Advocate, Strengthener, and Standby.

When Jesus said He was going away, He promised to send another *Comforter*. Have you ever tried Him out in that respect? I have. I remember one day when I was lonely, with my hands in dishwater and my girls away at school. I had a bad marriage situation. I was in a great big, nine room house by myself. The world was caving in on me. I was feeling sorry for myself. The Holy Spirit brought to my remembrance that He was the Comforter and the tears started trickling down my face as I said, "Lord, you said the Holy Spirit was a Comforter. Well, I'm in a state where I sure do need to be comforted. So come on, Holy Spirit, please comfort me!"

As soon as those words left my mouth the presence of the Lord engulfed me. I wasn't even aware of loneliness or of being alone. I was so caught up in the presence of God as I stood there with my hands still in the dishwater.

Do you know where that comfort came from? Not out of the blue somewhere. It came from the very core of my being, and just began to spring up and permeate the whole of me, and I just began to be locked in with Him.

The Holy Spirit is a *Counselor.* I like that because there are times when you want to talk to somebody, and you're afraid because they might tell it or not understand you. You need somebody who will be objective about your situation. The Lord through the Holy Spirit does love to sit down and talk with you and counsel with you! He does not counsel you apart from himself so if you want counsel, you have to enter into His presence.

The Holy Spirit is an *Intercessor.* That's why I like to pray in tongues. When I'm at my wit's end and something is going on that I don't understand, I begin to use my prayer language. Then the Spirit takes over to make intercession for me, the Scripture says, with unspeakable yearnings and groanings too deep for utterance (Rom. 8:26).

Have you ever been overwhelmed? Just full and brimming over, wanting to cry, not even knowing what you want to cry about? Then you begin to pray in your prayer language and all that heaviness, and whatever is

going on that you don't understand, is just lifted right out
of you as you go ahead to shed those tears. You find
yourself in the presence of God because the Holy Spirit
starts interceding through you. In order for the Holy
Spirit to intercede before God, He must be in the presence
of God. So what happens? He ushers *you* right into the
presence of God.

The Holy Spirit is our *Advocate.* He pleads our case
before the Father and defends us from the enemy accuser.

He is our *Strengthener,* who builds us up in our
weakness. We draw strength from the Lord each time we
get into His presence.

He will be our *Standby.* I need somebody who I know
is always standing there, especially since I am by myself a
whole lot. It's great just to know that somebody is with
you even though you can't touch Him; but He has a way of
letting you know every now and then, "Hey, I'm here. I'm
right here with you."

Once I had been very hurt. I was lying in bed crying and
I thought my heart was going to break. I never crawled up
on my own daddy's lap, but my grandfather used to hold
me in his lap. I can remember being upset when I was
already a young woman and granddaddy would say to me,
"Gal, how's the world treating you? What's going on?"
And I'd burst out crying and throw myself into his arms.

I never got too big to him. When I was twenty-five
years old I was still welcome to crawl up on my
granddaddy's lap. Even when I had three babies, he'd
take me and all three of them and hold us on his lap. And
me and all my kids would cry together.

God is my big Daddy. One day I was blue and the whole

bit before I realized that I didn't ever have to be that way. I was crying and there weren't any arms to hold me and not a lap for me to curl up in. I entered directly into the presence of God because God was my big Daddy. The whole room filled with the most glorious glow, just like a rosy fog. God literally rocked me to sleep in my bed in His arms like a little bitty kid because I was simple enough to get into His presence.

We miss so much because we don't know that we have the right to get into His presence anytime. Sometimes our husbands get so caught up with the things of the world, trying to make a living for us, and fighting that world out there, that they are not always mindful of the little things that we women need—those little attentions and touches. When you feel that nobody cares, and you desire a tender moment, and your husband is not available, Jesus is. You don't have to get mad at your husband. Don't give the enemy ANY GROUND by saying, "Well, he just doesn't care. All he cares about is making money and that job of his."

That's not true. He's working on that job to make it good for you and yours. He's doing the best that he knows how to do. When a man is occupied, he can't think about the little things. And we gals need the little things. Jesus said *He* would be to us whatever we need. We can simply pray, "Lord, I have a need for tenderness. I want a gentle touch, and John (or Philip or whatever your husband's name is) is so caught up in his work, but Lord, would you please make up for the deficiency that I feel in my relationship with him?" Do you know what Jesus will do? He'll usher you right into His presence and give you exactly what you need!

That doesn't apply only to women. Men know that women can get very preoccupied too. They get caught up with those babies, trying to keep house, cooking the meals and everything, to the extent that they are not aware that men need tenderness too. Men, instead of getting grouchy, pray, "Jesus, make up the difference for what Mary (or Helen, or Sue) can't give me right now." Do you know what? He'll usher you right into His presence because He is no respecter of persons (Acts. 10:34). Men, don't be so proud that you get your dander up and say, "I don't need that sort of thing!" Get to the place where you're willing to be tender, and recognize that you, too, need it. Get in touch with your feelings and get into the presence of God.

He is the *Holy Spirit*, and it is He who ushers us into the presence of God. Sometimes you get so worn out that you think you can't make it regardless of what you do—no matter how many saunas you take, or how many days you lie on the beach, or how many times you prop yourself up in front of the boob tube, or how many football games you watch, or whatever. You just can't seem to get refreshed and rid of that exhaustion. Get into the presence of God because "*there* are the times of refreshing, of reviving . . . in the presence of the Lord."

Do you know that any situation you are in is a divine "calling card" or invitation for you to come into the presence of God? We fight battles that we don't even need to fight. If we'd just get into the presence of God, He'd tell us that the battle is already won because He is the victor over everything!

David said, "Cause me to hear Your lovingkindness in the morning; for on You do I lean and in You do I trust. Cause me to know the way wherein I should walk, for I lift up my inner self to You" (Ps. 143:8).

What is your inner self? It is your spirit. David was saying that he wanted to know what God had for him to do that day. I want to know what I need for this day. I want to walk with God and to be taught His way. I realize that I can't discover these things apart from God so I'm going to lift myself, my spirit, right up into God's presence, and He will teach me in my inner self.

The Word says that the name of the Lord is like a strong tower, and we are safe, high above evil, and strong if we run into it (Prov. 18:10). Have you ever run unto Jesus? That's getting into His presence where you will be safe.

"You are my hiding place and my shield" (Ps. 119:114). Have you settled it that God is your hiding place? Paul tells us that our life is hid with Christ in God (Col. 3:3). Have you settled your security in Him?

David said, "You are my refuge in times of trouble" (Ps. 9:9). Whenever there is a storm in your life and the winds start blowing and things get rough, that's the time to run into the presence of God. That's *not* the time to try to handle it yourself or try to muster up your own strength. Go where you know your help comes from. That's the time to *run* into the presence of God!

We are promised in Psalm 91 that God would hide us in the midst of pestilence and destruction and that it wouldn't be able to come near our dwelling place. Why? Because God would hover over us and hide us under the shadow of His wings. Oh, if we'd just learn how to run into

His presence!

David said, "Deliver me, O Lord, from my enemies; I flee to You to hide me" (Ps. 143:9). I never try to protect myself because it is Jesus who is my shield and my buckler. He is my rod and my staff, symbols of comfort (Ps. 23).

"And in your mercy and lovingkindness cut off my enemies and destroy all those who afflict my inner self, for I am Your servant" (Ps. 143:12). When I read that passage, I could hardly believe it for joy. I began to think about the enemies that afflict *my inner self*, that afflict my spirit. What kind of enemies would they be? Anxieties, fears, bitterness, anger, resentments, all of which cause physical manifestations of sickness, tensions, and worry. We fight these outside things, but God says, "Flee into my presence."

If you flee into His presence with all of your anxiety, you'll find the Word of God effective: "Do not fret or have any anxiety about anything, but in every circumstance and in everything by prayer and petition [definite requests] with thanksgiving continue to make your wants known to God" (Phil. 4:6). What happens to your anxiety in the presence of God? It disappears!

If you hate someone (and as a believer you know you shouldn't hate anybody, but still that old hate is bugging you), don't get upset because you can't get rid of hate by yourself. Take that hate and run with it into the presence of Jesus. What's going to happen to that hate? Go and see!

Fear is something the enemy uses to afflict our inward self. If you fear, you are tormented. Don't try to fight it or even to pray it away. Just take your fear and run into the presence of God. There won't be any place for it there!

You may experience that sometimes you start praying in your prayer language, but once you get into the presence of God, your prayer language ceases. You don't even need to say anything. You begin that spirit to Spirit communication, and something starts happening on the inside because you are in the presence of God. Joy begins to fill and flood your whole being.

You can't stay in the presence of God for two minutes and come out the same as you went in. When you behold Him, and He looks at you, there is a beautiful exchange. He puts His image into you. He sees himself because we are His mirrors. A mirror only reflects the likeness of the one who is looking into it. When we get into His presence, we receive the assurance that we're God's kids, and when we come out, we can lick the world through Him.

If we even try to remember what problem drove us there, it seems so inconsequential. Now you can hold your head high, your shoulders straighten up, and you know who you are. You look at the person who was bugging you and you just begin to love them. You didn't know they were so beautiful! *They* aren't any different, but now you are looking out of the eyes of Jesus.

Do you want to know a secret? The enemy can't stand in the presence of God. He already knows he's defeated and that Jesus is victor over him. When you get into the presence of God, you leave the enemy standing right outside the door—there is no way he can go in with you! That is a *sure* way to GIVE NO GROUND to the enemy!

What a great reason to learn how to walk, talk, run, play, worship, drive, cook, eat, and sleep in the presence of God! Learn how to live all the time in His presence and the enemy will have NO GROUND in you!

I get up every morning and go through the usual routine of bathing, dressing, and asking the Lord to pick out my clothes. Then I say, "Lord, I have taken care of that which I can handle. Now I want you to put on me the *spiritual equipment and adornments* that I will need for today because only you know what kind of situations and battles I'm going to be in mentally, emotionally, morally, physically, academically, socially, everything. You dress me on the *inside* like I have taken care of the *outside*.

Then I continue in His presence all day fully aware that I've got it all together and I go ahead and simply live in Him.

21

SPEEDING ON OUR HORSES

It must puzzle God (though of course, being all-knowing, He is not surprised at anything) that His children prefer speeding on their own horses instead of resting in confidence in His almighty strength.

"In returning to Me . . . shall be your strength. And you would not, But you said, No! We will speed on our own course on horses!" (Isa. 30:15, 16).

Toddlers who are just acquiring their first few vocabulary words often attack little tasks that are beyond their maturity with their insistence on, "Me do! Me do!" We either smile or frown as they fumble and fail. But look at us—we get bucked off our "speeding horses" too, (whatever they are in our lives) but God just keeps loving us and teaching us about trusting Him instead. And trusting Him means rest. Why is that so hard?

Many believers are still striving for what God has already given as a gift. The enemy of our souls does not want us to know that we already have rest, because he gains a lot of GROUND from our not knowing it.

The fourth chapter of Hebrews tells us about entering into rest and learning how to trust God. The writer tells us we should labor to enter into the rest, but that once we have entered it, we should cease from our own labors. It's not that we don't work any more, but that we don't do *our own thing* any more; we become consumed with the desire to do the will of the Father.

"Let us therefore be zealous and exert ourselves and strive diligently to enter into that rest[of God]—to know and experience it for ourselves . . . for he who has once entered into [God's] rest also has ceased from [the weariness and pain] of human labors, just as God rested from those labors peculiarly His own" (Heb. 4:11, 10).

"For thus said the Lord God, the Holy One of Israel, In returning to Me and resting in Me you shall be saved; in quietness and in (trusting) confidence shall be your strength. And you would not, *But you said, No! We will speed on our own course on horses!*" (Isa. 30:15, 16). Does that sound familiar in our experience?

Jesus said similar yearning words when He sat and looked over Jerusalem. He wept with tender love: "O Jerusalem, Jerusalem. . . . How often would I have gathered your children together as a mother fowl gathers her brood under her wings, and you refused!" (Matt. 23:37).

When you really know who you are, and you really know what you possess, you can relax and rest. You don't have to panic when difficult situations come up because Paul assured us so beautifully, "*All* things work together and are[fitting into a plan] for good to those who love God and are called according to [His] design and purpose"

(Rom. 8:28). It is not just one thing, or the things you can understand, or the things that you can handle, or approve of—but *all* things. That includes the good, the bad, and the seemingly neutral or indifferent.

Nothing makes the enemy more angry than for you to ignore him, look past him and see Jesus. Especially when he has gone to all the trouble to throw an obstacle in your way, and you insist on standing there and dealing with God directly: "Hey God, please tell me what this means." The enemy wanted your attention on himself. He wishes you would say, "Oh, I'm so upset; the devil has thrown this obstacle in my way!" The enemy can't get any mileage out of trouble if your mind and heart are fixed on Jesus. He LOSES GROUND.

I learned to trust the Lord in the little, practical everyday experiences. After praying a simple prayer of surrender each morning, asking the Lord to take over everything, I just live. If I find myself turning an unexpected corner and going in a direction different from what I've planned, I don't panic and start biting my nails. I just say, "Okay, Lord, what are you saying to me? What do you want me to do or learn?" Or "Whom can I help while I'm here?"

I'm a firm believer that there are no mistakes, no ifs, ands, buts, or maybes in Jesus. He said that "in quietness and in confidence shall be your strength."

After you have returned to God, the thing to do is rest and trust Him with what you've given Him. What have you given Him? Your life, your possessions, everything you know how to give Him. If there's anything more that He needs, an area that you haven't exposed to Him, it is the work of the Holy Spirit to disclose it to you. When He does reveal it, simply say, "Lord, I'm sorry. Forgive me. Here—I offer this to your lordship." Don't take it as condemnation. Just keep on walking. That's resting; that's trusting.

God told the Israelites not to go back to Egypt and trust in their chariots again (2 Kings 18:21, 24). After we have given ourselves to the Lord, we are not to go back to trusting in anything that we have, no matter how good it is—our minds, our own talents, or abilities, or whatever we had before. "Put your trust and confidence only in me," God says.

I have already mentioned the heart attack I had a number of years ago when I made the exchange of my little faith with God's great faithfulness.

I had been working hard to keep my oldest child in school, which was part of the reason I got sick. I knew there was something radically wrong, but I wouldn't give in to it. One morning I just couldn't move or raise my arm. I had tremendous pain. The only thing I could whisper was, "Help!" My youngest girl was at home and she phoned my mom. When I got to the doctor he already had the nurses and the stretcher ready. They shot me in both arms and rushed me into an oxygen tent. The doctor told my mother that I had a fifty-fifty chance, and he didn't know which way it was going. My mother began to sob and panic at the foot of my bed.

My youngest girl, who was fourteen at the time, looked at my mom and said, "Stop all this fussing. Don't you know that my mother is a child of God, and He's going to take care of her?" I heard that just as I was drifting off to

172

sleep from the medication. I thanked God that regardless of what happened, I had lived in front of my girls so that they knew God was a reality and that He was my God.

Little did I know that I was moving at that time into the center of the rest of God because I had reached the place where it just *didn't make any difference*. If I got well, it was okay; if I didn't get well, it was all right too. Jesus was in control!

When you know what you know, and you know who you are, and you know that God has your life, and you've made Him Lord over your life, why should you struggle to save something that is not even your own? The Word of God says that you have been bought with a price, so you don't belong to yourself (1 Cor. 6:19, 20). That price is the shed blood of Jesus Christ.

While I was in the hospital, I went on a fast because I was doing business with the Lord. The people would come from the big ward to see the lady in the oxygen tent because I was teaching and preaching faith. I would pray for people and lay hands on them. God was healing some and sending them home while I was still lying sick in an oxygen tent.

I'd ask, "Where is that lady who came down yesterday?"

They'd answer, "Something really strange happened. Everything suddenly got normal and the doctors sent her home."

There was a gal in the room who was having shock treatments. Every time she found herself getting really nervous, she'd run to my bed, shake my tent, and cry, "Pray! Pray! Pray!" And I'd start praying. The patients wouldn't go to sleep unless I prayed every night. I prayed for everybody before I'd go to sleep. Then I'd pray when I woke up in the morning so we'd have a good day. I'd pray for the doctors and nurses to have wisdom to know the best to do for us all and that they would accept Jesus.

All kinds of things were happening while *I* was lying in an oxygen tent worrying about *losing my faith!* I didn't have sense enough to know at that time that God was *increasing the very thing* that I was crying out to Him about, because what I was doing was acting on what *little* faith I had.

After the Lord had accomplished what He wanted, there and in me, God finally released me from the oxygen tent and I went home.

It is God's responsibility to take care of your life, your daily food, your place to live, and your clothes to wear. He said, "But seek for (aim at and strive after) first of all His kingdom, and His righteousness [His way of doing and being right], and then all these things taken together will be given you besides" (Matt. 6:33). Jesus said that your heavenly Father knows that you have need of all the things of daily life that are so practical. He's the Lord God, the Jehovah-Jireh of the Old Testament, who provides. Though for the moment your situation might look like a terrible disaster, either His Word is true that *all* things are working together for good, or He is a liar.

One reason why I admonish you to study the Word of God so intensely is that you can remind God of what He has said in a time of crisis. He delights in watching over His Word, hastening to perform it. He really, *really*, REALLY wants to perform His Word, but He needs people to channel it through who believe His Word to the point that they will trust Him and move out with it.

22

MORE ABOUT REST

I have a definition for REST. I feel it is very realistic. It is R-I-S-K. When you get to the point where you're not afraid to risk anything, *then* you're willing to rest in the Lord and trust Him with everything you have.

Hebrews 4 not only talks about entering into rest, but it goes on to tell you what that word is all about. What is our confidence? It is a Person; our confidence is a Man; our confidence is in the Word made flesh: Jesus Christ. When you look at Jesus, you don't find failure. Do you see any situation in which Jesus failed? Then it is logical to conclude that *Jesus in you* will not fail!

God the Father said over and over again that He is the Lord our God who fails not (Jer. 32:27; Deut. 31:6; Heb. 13:5). If Jesus didn't fail and He was the manifestation of God the Father, who promises not to fail, why should *you* accept failure? Fear is perfect faith in failure. Some believers are so sure that they are going to fail that they can't succeed. The enemy has a LOT OF GROUND when he binds you to your fear of failure. He will cause you just to sit there on your stool and do nothing.

We learn some very important things about the Word of God: "For the Word that God speaks is alive and full of power—making it active, operative, energizing and effective; it is sharper than any two-edged sword, penetrating to the dividing line of the breath of life (soul) and [the immortal] spirit, and of joints and marrow [that is, of the deepest parts of our nature] exposing and sifting and analyzing and judging the very thoughts and purposes of the heart" (Heb. 4:12). The Word separates—even between such delicate things as the bone from the marrow, which is the blood and the life of the bone.

When we enter into the rest of God, it is His Word in our hearts that lets us know whether or not we are total in our relationship with Him. How fragmented many of us Christians still are! But the Word of God will make us whole persons so that we can respond to Him and to our circumstances in wholeness.

In order to rest, you have to trust. There's a gospel song with the words, "Laid out on Jesus; laid way back in His love." But most of us don't trust Him enough to lie fully on Him; we'll lean on Him a little and we think that we've really done something. We're contented if we can sing sincerely, "Leaning on the everlasting arms," but it's another thing to lie down close in them. But that's exactly where the Lord wants us.

When a professional swimmer gets a cramp, the first thing he does is to relax and lie down restfully on the water and float. He doesn't panic and struggle. That's a fantastic illustration of learning to rest in the Lord.

What counts is not our efforts, but what He can do. We should let Him call the shots until His life in us becomes the current that carries us where we need to go. If we never get to the place of resting on Him, how will we ever find out that He cares so much for us? The Scripture says to strive to get into the rest; whatever it costs, get there, be willing to pay it. But once you get there, we are told, relax!

When you go to the doctor with a pain, the first thing he tells you is to relax. Do you know that you can endure more pain by relaxing than you can by getting all uptight and steeling yourself against it? The doctor can't even find what's bothering you if you are uptight, especially if you have some problem in your abdomen.

When you begin to trust and rest, it will build your confidence. I have found out that God doesn't just do what is best for *me*, but for everything that concerns me and the lives that I touch. Sometimes that means I might have to die to what I want so that the good of *everybody* will be received.

The key to resting is knowing where to go. God said, "Don't panic and run to Egypt to get your help—that's where you were and it didn't help you." God doesn't want us to run somewhere else first and then come back to Him as a last resort. Run to your source first. It seems to be the hardest thing to do to learn to depend on Jesus, because we've been taught to be independent and capable in ourselves. We are told that if we don't do it, who is going to do it for us? We think we have to work. The Lord says, "Come to me *first*."

I used to go to the Lord after I had exhausted everything else. I had to get a new attitude like everyone else. I had to get reprogramed that "Without Me (Jesus) you can do nothing." If I can't do anything, why not go directly and promptly to the One who *can do everything*? I found myself putting new thoughts into my computer.

I had been a mother for a long time before I discovered that I didn't know how to be one. I had to have help from God to be a mother.

I'd been a sister all my life, but I had to ask the Lord how to be a sister—and how to be a wife—and how to be a daughter. I realized I really didn't know anything on my own.

Everything I had learned, including my concepts about Jesus, I had learned from men, from the church. And I wanted to know the whole truth, God's pure truth. I had to give up everything that I knew so that I could find out the truth because there was a conflict inside me. The Holy Spirit was showing me one thing, and my loyalties and my concepts and my traditions were going in another direction.

God said, "Well, Ev, you have to get rid of everything that you know." Now that is scary.

There were some things I was confident in. I thought I could really rest in those things. But God repeated, "Ev, you have to give it *all* up. Even your own ideas about morals."

"Morals?" I said.

He said, "Yeah, morals. So that I can teach you what *is* the truth."

Do you realize that everything you've been taught, you've been taught by a person, and not every person who taught you was of God. God said, "Even the common things your mother taught you, if she didn't know me, may not have been the truth. She was under the lordship of the enemy." That was kind of scary too. But God insisted, "Everything!"

Do you know what we adults do? We pass on our prejudices and old wives' tales to our children as truth. We have received hang ups, and then we pass them right on to the next generation. And we teach these things as though they were gospel. Our kids end up being hung-up with the same old hang ups that have been passed down for years on end.

I've had people say to me, "Well, after all, I'm Irish and all Irishmen have quick tempers; therefore, naturally I'm supposed to have a bad temper."

I ask, "Are you a born-again believer in Jesus Christ?"

"Yeah."

"Spirit-filled?"

"Uh-huh."

"And you have license to have a temper because you are a child of the Irish?" I said, "I thought you were a child of God."

Even our heritage can become a stumbling block to our relationship with Jesus. If you really trust God, then you're willing to let go of everything in order to find out what the truth is all about.

For example, your idea of being a man. Your dad taught you how to be a man and he told you that "men don't cry." You learned how to suppress your emotions from the time you were a little fellow. If you hurt yourself and your bottom lip began to quiver, your dad said, "Now be a man!"

You said, "I'm going to be a man if it kills me!" Do you wonder why you can never get in touch with your feelings? Because you can't handle your feelings, a lot of you toss your feelings aside. You are afraid of your own gentleness and tenderness. Why? Because you have been programed that to cry is feminine. But it takes a real man to be able to cry. "Manliness" does not mean being stoical, possessing sexual potency, and having the ability to lift weights. Doubtless Jesus himself cried on many other occasions beside the few that are recorded in Scripture. Some of the strongest men I have ever met have been the most gentle and sensitive men. They don't feel threatened by the expression of their emotions. They have centered them in God.

We can never rest in God by carrying the same old ideas and concepts into our Christian lives. If we are going to trust Him, we have to let go of everything and find out what His truth is all about. Do you know what comes with that? Great confidence!

Some people have said to me, "Evelyn, you're the most arrogant black woman that I have ever seen."

I reply, "I'm not arrogant; I'm just confident in Jesus!"

When you know that you know, you know that you know. You don't have to worry about being shaken. So the writer of Hebrews tells us, "Whatever the cost, labor to get into the rest of God."

How would you begin to get into the rest of God? You start with choice. I choose to enter His rest. I choose to lay everything down in order to find God's truth. Then everything will come directly from God and the enemy will have NO GROUND in you because he doesn't have power over anything of God's!

When you give up all of your past concepts to rest in Him, God may still pick and choose from your past (which He certainly had a hand in, even before you knew Him) if something can be used for His glory. That's up to Him.

For example, from the time I was a little child, I had the ability to talk—the gift of gab. So I decided I wanted to be an attorney. I wanted to be the first black woman criminal lawyer. I wanted to study law and practice it in Chicago, because, at that time, that city was a seat of crime.

Circumstances did not allow me to become an attorney. When God called me into the ministry, He said, "Evelyn, you always wanted to be a lawyer. Well now, you're going to be *my attorney*. Satan is going to be your opponent. You're going to win your case over him at every turn because *I'm the judge*. But you're not going to do something just for black people. You're going to do something for *all* my people."

God took that gift of gab from my past and redeemed it to use for the praise of His glory. When we offer our lives to Jesus, and surrender all that we have to Him, He redeems the whole of us and it is up to Him what He wants to use. Resting in Him means just that—that we leave it up to Him to call the shots!

23

DON'T FORGET
TO FORGET

We've been dealing with many things to *remember* so that the enemy would have NO GROUND. *Forgetting* is important too. Let's work up to it.

This is one of my favorite passages: "But whatever former things I had that might have been gains to me, I have come to consider as (one combined) loss for Christ's sake.

"Yes, furthermore I count everything as loss compared to the possession of the priceless privilege—the overwhelming preciousness . . . of knowing Christ Jesus my Lord, and of progressively becoming more deeply and intimately acquainted with Him, of perceiving and recognizing and understanding Him more fully and clearly. For His sake I have lost everything and consider it all to be mere rubbish (refuse, dregs), in order that I may win (gain) Christ, the Anointed One" (Phil. 3:7, 8).

We often have our eyes mainly on the benefits a relationship will give us. We want to be filled with the

Holy Spirit so that we can receive His gifts. We want to know more about the Lord so that our needs might be fulfilled. But Paul said, *"I want to know Him."* He was not so much interested in all the fringe benefits as he was in getting to know more about Christ.

Don't get so caught up in the *gifts*; get truly caught up with the *giver*. The gifts are going to operate anyway as a result of who you are. But fall in love with Jesus. To me Christianity is a love affair with Him. Moment by moment, day by day, have a hunger to know Him more intimately.

Be willing to turn away from anything that distracts or interferes with developing that relationship. If there is a pleasure, or a habit that interferes with your relationship with Jesus, then ask the Lord to help you get rid of it. It doesn't matter how good it is. The enemy of your soul can GAIN GROUND from it.

Not only did Paul want to know Him, but he longed for him: "that I may [actually] be found and known as in Him, not having any (self-achieved) righteousness that can be called my own, based on my obedience to the Law's demands—ritualistic uprightness and [supposed] right standing with God thus acquired—but possessing that [genuine righteousness] which comes through faith in Christ, the Anointed One, the [truly] right standing with God, which comes from God by (saving) faith" (Phil.3:9).

The Word of God says that it is "not because of works, lest any man should boast" (Eph. 2:9). It's by faith. For us to receive the grace of God in vain so that it is of no effect is grieving to the heart and the mind of God. But to be found in Christ, hid in God, and our actions and reactions motivated out of our love relation for Him, will let the world know that our Christ is a living reality.

Paul goes on to say: [For my determined purpose is] that I may know Him—that I may progressively become more deeply and intimately acquainted with Him, perceiving and recognizing and understanding [the wonders of His Person] more strongly and more clearly. And that I may in that same way come to know the power outflowing from His resurrection [which it exerts over believers]; . . . [even while in the body]" (Phil. 3:10, 11).

The resurrection life of Jesus Christ has power *right now* in the life of the believer. There is power in Jesus and it's the "all power" of Matt. 28:18 that was given to Him—and to *us* through Him.

Paul said that one thing he was going to do is to *forget* what was behind (v. 13). One of the biggest stumbling blocks among Christians is that we don't forget what lies behind. We become new creatures in Christ Jesus (2 Cor. 5:17), and this becomes our testimony. But somehow we can't forget what we have been. Does the enemy bring up your past to plague you when you want to pray or lay hands on someone for healing? Settle it—the past is *forgiven* in Jesus and should be *forgotten* by us too.

There are diversities of ministries in the body of Christ. I believe that not everybody needs a healing of memories. This is a very active and important ministry today and has a definite place in the body; but, I don't think everybody needs it. The normal thing is to simply accept the power of the shed blood of Jesus Christ and not to go back into one's past to dig up things to get free of them. We can, if the Holy Spirit brings up something specific, lift it up immediately into the light of His love, asking Him by His power and His Spirit to cleanse us of it and the ties that it has on us emotionally, mentally, morally, and physically. We should let the blood do the work without necessarily going back and scrounging around in it. Paul simply said, "Forgetting. . . ."

We have to forget with the whole personality—with our minds, our wills, and our emotions. Usually when we are tied to the past it is in our emotions. Because we have not lifted up and exposed that area to the Lord Jesus Christ, we are fragmented. In our emotions we start remembering what we were, and the enemy has a field day with us. We believe his lie. We don't accept God's fact that we are new creatures in Christ Jesus, and that old things *have* passed away, and *all* things have become new.

Don't look backward. You can't progress with your head twisted around looking where you have been. Paul said, "I just forget it." Choose to pray, "Now, Lord, bring my emotions up to the level of that truth so that I can move on."

We have to forget before we can "strain forward to what lies ahead, I press on toward the goal to win the [supreme and heavenly] prize to which God in Christ Jesus is calling us upward" (Phil 3:13, 14). The Lord is constantly beckoning to us: "Come on; move on; exercise yourself; stretch yourself." It's a progressive life in the Spirit. We just grow and grow and grow.

Paul said that "We possess this precious treasure in vessels of earth that the grandeur and exceeding greatness of the power may be shown to be of God and not from ourselves" (2 Cor. 4:7). The treasure is in the vessel. Is it the receptacle that possesses the treasure, or the treasure that possesses the receptacle? Which is the precious part?

We're so busy polishing the outside rather than allowing the treasure that is within us to have the prominent place. We should develop this treasure so that it permeates and takes over and shines forth from and through that vessel. It is the treasure, Christ in us, that makes the vessel important. We're busy painting and fixing up these old clay pots trying to make them worthy of the treasure. It's the stuff on the inside that makes the clay pot worthwhile and holy and attractive. We so easily get off center in our priorities.

God never works from the circumference to the center; always from the center to the circumference. The Spirit of God works in us, refining us, making us sensitive and more like Jesus.

When God looks upon the earth, do you know what He expects to see? Nothing less than a reflection of himself in our clay pots. We are in the process of being changed more and more into the image and likeness of Christ who is in us by the Spirit as we behold Him in the Word of God (2 Cor. 3:18).

God is interested in developing character not making reputations. Man will give you a reputation. He can take it away too. But God is developing Christ-like character, just like himself. All of the attributes which were in Christ are to be manifested in the lives of those who have received Jesus as Lord (Rom. 8:29).

Let's forget about what has been. Let's begin to

cooperate with Him who is on the inside, whom we have invited to be Lord. Let's allow Him to be Lord over everything that touches us. We need to reach the point where we declare that everything we have is as garbage that we might gain the excellency and the knowledge of Christ.

I like that old song that we've sung in my church since I was a little girl: "Nothing between my soul and the Savior." The cry in the heart and mind of every believer should be: "Lord, I don't want anything between you and me. Jesus, if there's something wrong in me, by the power of your Holy Spirit, reveal it."

The Word says we stand naked before God (Heb. 4:13). If God already knows everything about us, why should we put on a sham? Don't let the enemy TAKE GROUND through deceiving thoughts like, *Well, as soon as you get rid of this, you might become a worker for the Lord.* Clear up all that you know to be wrong between you and the Lord, but don't wait around until you think you are perfect before you serve the Lord. God doesn't wait to use us until we are *good* enough; He uses us when we are *available.*

One of the things that is so terribly grieving and insulting to the Lord is that when He has already forgiven us at so great a cost, we refuse to forgive ourselves. We get the idea that if the Lord doesn't punish us, we'll have to punish ourselves. So we begin the flagellation. We say, "No, thank you," to the mercies of God because we've decided we're not good enough to receive them.

We never will be, but we are made worthy (Eph. 2:13). He took our filthy unrighteousness which He said was like filthy rags (Isa. 64:6), and gave us His righteousness as a robe to clothe us (Isa. 61:10). There we stand before the Father presented faultless, blameless, guiltless, moment by moment (Eph. 5:27; Col. 1:22; Jude 24). When God looks at us, it is through the blood of Jesus and He sees us as righteous, holy, pure.

We need to learn to look at ourselves in the same way He looks at us. So, forget the past.

The Word of God tells us, "Love your neighbor as [you do] yourself" (Matt. 22:39). The reason some of us can't love our neighbors is because we don't love ourselves. We have such a poor self-image. How do you dare have a poor self-image when it cost God so much to give you a new one? Forget it, forget it! Choose to think about yourself the way Jesus thinks about you.

It's not going to be easy, but it's simple. I'd much rather think about myself in the manner that the Lord thinks about me than to struggle to keep my old mind-set. It's so freeing. You can hold your head up. Scripture says, "If the Son liberates you—makes you free men—then you are really and unquestionably free" (John 8:36). Free from the bondage of old emotions, free from the bondage of frustration, anger, resentment, and bitterness. Free to grow and become all that God says we are. Then when He needs someone to minister through, we're available. We can say, "Lord, here I am" (Isa. 6:8).

"Will you go lay hands on that person?"

"Yes, Lord."

Supposing the enemy will say, "Do you think you're good enough?"

"Yes, through the blood of Jesus, I am. I'm just going as

His hands."

The Scripture says, "Always be ready to give a logical defense to any one who asks you to account for the hope that is in you" (1 Pet. 3:15). That includes answering the enemy when he comes at you. You ought to be sure who you are and ready to counter him with the Word of God because you have spent time in the Word.

The Bible tells us that we are partakers and sharers of the divine nature (2 Pet. 1:4). Am I good enough? Yes. How do I know? I have His nature. Oh, does that make the enemy mad!

Somebody might say, "Oh, you think you're God, don't you?"

"No, but I have His Spirit."

Somebody else might say, "You make me so mad! Every time I see you, you're grinning. What do you have to be so happy about?" Then you have a chance to run down the things you have to be happy about in Jesus.

Or they'll remind you, "Don't you see all the terrible things that are going on in the world?"

"Yes, it's my Daddy's world. Did you notice it too? He's taking care of it."

Let your testimony be *so sure*. The Word says, "Make sure your calling and election; for if you do this you will never stumble or fall" (2 Pet. 1:10). And the enemy will have NO GROUND in you!

We've been elected by God himself to be His! Why should we grovel and groan? If we only knew the half of what we are in Christ, we'd be shouting all day! Doesn't all of this sound great to you? I think I just grew ten feet tall! If I declare a few more of these wonderful things to you, I might explode. I'm finding out who I am myself. I thought I knew, but I am still finding out more!

I love to read the Scriptures to find out what I possess. I'm always finding some extras that belong to me. God *wants* us to lay claim to His promises.

There's a song that goes, "Every promise in the Book is *mine*; Every chapter, every verse, every line." I got to thinking, "Yeah, that really is so! Written for Evelyn!" Written for you!

Do you know what the Bible is? A love letter from home! We are pilgrims traveling in a far country looking for a city. Only *we* know where we're going, don't we? We're looking for the new Jerusalem but we don't have to look in vain because it is going to find *us*!

Abraham died hoping. He kept the faith and he searched and he looked. But *we* don't have to die just hoping; we've received! Jesus has already gone to the cross and secured our salvation. We *know* where we're going.

So we ought to know who we are, too. I'm a citizen of God's kingdom. All the rights of the kingdom are mine. I have a temporary dwelling place here, but I have another one in heaven. I'm a citizen of two places. I can have the best of this land and the best that is in the land to come. How can you have a hangdog look when you have everything going for you? Right now, and after a while, and by-and-by too!

Follow on to know the Lord. Get so hungry and excited when you read the Scriptures that you can't get enough of them. There's a promise for me to learn! Here's a sin I'm being convicted of. Or there's something I'm going to be able to claim today. Man, I want to see what is mine *today* because I can stand that much taller as soon as I find it. I put my finger on the promise and say, "Father, in the name of Jesus, I claim it. *This is mine.* Now it's up to you to make it real to me because I believe you and I'm going to walk in the light of it."

Forget what you were before you read this book. You'll be different when you finish it because your attitude will be changed. Why? Because of the enlightenment of the Word. People are going to notice a difference in you. You'll look different. You'll have a lilt in your step. God is doing something inside of you that is going to be manifested on the outside. You are learning to give NO GROUND to the enemy!

24

STAND TALL
IN ME, JESUS

I used to be a striving Christian. I was determined to be
the best Baptist Christian you could find. I was going to
do it if it killed me. And it nearly did! I was so busy
striving and struggling to do everything just right that I
lost the real perspective of God's truth.

I was going to teach my daughters culture by hook or by
crook. I saw to it that they all had their little patent
leather shoes, their white gloves, their little straw hats,
their natty navy blue coats. I always took them to "the
finer things." We were first-nighters at the theater. I
taught them what curtain calls were, what the overture
was, and all that sort of stuff.

They tell stories about me now. They say, "You know,
momma was really tough on us!"

I figured little girls were supposed to stand tall and be
very feminine. I had one daughter who walked a little
bent over—slouchy, you know. Now I don't ever
remember this, but they insist that I did it.

195

"Do you remember how momma used to put her knee in our backs? 'Straighten up!' she shouted."

I said, "You're puttin' me on."

"Honest, momma, you were always straightening us up. Even when we were walking down the street with our little pocketbooks and gloves, you walked right up and stuck your knee in our backs!

"Momma, you just don't remember some of the things you used to do!"

That's *some* of the things *I* like to forget. I was so rigid. But that's where I was in my development at that particular time. I thought all of this was being holy and was going to make me sanctified.

But when the Lord made me holy it had nothing to do with all the external rules that I kept and all my striving and foolishness. Jesus did an inside job in my heart. Before, I had been hard and bitter and angry because I could never really express myself. I was always uptight.

When I really came to know Jesus, I found out that a lot of the things that I had been taught as tradition in my church had nothing whatever to do with my personal salvation. The length of my dress, whether I braided my hair or whether I curled it, whether I wore lipstick or whether I didn't, or where I went for my recreation—this had nothing to do with my standing before God. Salvation has to do with the heart, not with this other stuff.

After I got free in Jesus, the young people used to come to me and ask, "Should we do this? Can't we do that? How do you feel about this?"

I would tell them, "Get what I've got in Jesus and you won't have to worry about it." I said, "The Lord on the

inside will tell you whether it pleases Him or not." It's His
job to perfect His own. All the things that we can do
externally will never accomplish it. Only the things that
we permit Him to do in our lives cause us to become what
He would have us be.

We're all in the process of becoming. We can get awfully
hung-up trying to help Him out. We figure, "If I quit
doing this or that . . . ." But if you don't have the
conviction in your heart to quit something that's wrong,
you are trying to quit in the flesh. Once the Spirit of God
convicts you, you don't have to worry about whether a
thing is right or wrong and you don't need anybody to
approve of it either.

When I really fell in love with Jesus, I became very free
and very light and joyful. So joyful that one of the
"mothers" of the church came to see me one day. We did
polite stuff for a while and I gave her tea and all that.
When she got ready to leave, I said to her, "Shall we
pray?" She indulged me though I could see it was strange
to her. Young women were not supposed to act like I was
acting.

Then she said, "Daughter, just before I go, I really
want to tell you what I came for. You know, when you talk
about Jesus," she said, "your eyes sparkle and you get a
light in your face." She stood there patting me.
"Daughter, I'm so afraid you're going to be sick. . . ."
That's what she told me! I couldn't believe it.

I said, *"What?"*

She continued sympathetically, "I just want to warn
you to take it slow, honey, 'cause I'm so afraid. . . ." She
really was convinced that I was losing my mind because

197

NO GROUND

surely nobody could be as happy as I was or do the things I was doing unless she were bordering on crazy. No young woman was supposed to *like* to pray and fast and share Jesus. That was not normal by traditional church standards.

Well, if I did have a sickness and a dread disease, it was chronic because it never went away. And I guess it was contagious too! I can't help but be what I am because Jesus is working on me according to His blueprint. Maybe I do grin and bounce and get excited about Jesus, but I sort of think He likes me this way!

One girl walked up to me and said, "Evelyn, when you talk about the Lord that way, it's just like I feel about my husband!"

Another said, "When you get through preaching, I want to say, 'May I have a piece too? May I have a bite?' It sounds so good!"

We are the only witnesses for Jesus that people are going to see today. In order for them to know the reality of Jesus, *we* have to have the reality of Jesus. Do you know why? *Everybody in the Bible is dead!* Moses is dead; Matthew is dead; Mark is dead; so are Miriam, Lydia, and Mary. Everybody except Jesus! God needs some twentieth-century witnesses to the reality of His Word! He needs modern Marks, Pauls, Peters, Marys, and Lydias. And God, in His infinite mercy, through Jesus Christ, has chosen *us*. He said, "But you shall receive power when the Holy Spirit has come upon you; and you shall be My witnesses. . . ." Where? "In Jerusalem and all Judea and Samaria and to the ends—the very bounds— of the earth" (Acts 1:8). Right at home, in your

198

neighborhood and at the same time spreading Jesus abroad to all nations.

All you have to do is live in relationship with Jesus, and let the Word of God dwell in you richly (Col. 3:16), and be rooted and grounded in the faith. There will be an outward manifestation. People will want to know what makes you tick. Then you can tell them about Jesus. Praise the Lord!

So forget the things that are behind. Forget what you have been and stop trying to prove what you are. It's the *Lord's* privilege to prove truth. So forget emotionally, forget mentally, forget by the choice of your will. Forget what's behind you and start pressing to the mark of the high calling in Christ Jesus. If you don't remember anything else, remember to *be* like Jesus—BE like Jesus! That's the guarantee that the enemy won't have ANY GROUND in you, because he didn't have ANY GROUND in Jesus!

Paul said he was showing us a mystery that had been hidden for ages and generations from angels and men, but is now revealed: *"Christ within you the hope of glory"* (Col. 1:26, 27). And then he declared that in Christ all the fullness of the Godhead dwelled bodily (Col. 2:9, 10). And that *in Him* you are made full, and *reach full spiritual stature.* If you're full, and if you're *in Him* and He's *in you,* instead of trying to *be like* Him, why not *let Him be himself in you?* Delight to show Him off to the world as He shines out through you.

NO GROUND

Dear Jesus, here I am.
  Love through my heart.
  Think through my mind.
  Hear through my ears.
  See through my eyes.
  Speak through my lips.
  Touch through my hands.
  Walk through my feet.
Stand tall in me, Jesus, and do greater works
than you did when you were on the earth.

                       Amen

For free information on how to receive
the international magazine

LOGOS JOURNAL

also Book Catalog

Write: Information - LOGOS JOURNAL CATALOG
Box 191
Plainfield, NJ 07061